# Treasury of
# Early American
# Automobiles

—◦⸰❖⸰◦—

## 1877 = 1925

*Books Written and Published by Floyd Clymer:*

HISTORICAL MOTOR SCRAPBOOK

*(6 volumes)*

HISTORY OF AMERICAN STEAM AUTOMOBILES

ALBUM OF HISTORICAL STEAM TRACTION ENGINES

HISTORY OF ALL INDIANAPOLIS RACES

EARLY AUTO RACING IN AMERICA

MODERN FOREIGN AUTOMOBILES

MOTORING THROUGH EUROPE WITH CLYMER

*Treasury of*

# EARLY AMERICAN
# AUTOMOBILES

*1877 - 1925*

*by*

## FLOYD CLYMER

BONANZA BOOKS · NEW YORK

TREASURY OF EARLY AMERICAN AUTOMOBILES
1877–1925

*Copyright* MCML, *by Floyd Clymer*

This edition published by Bonanza Books
a division of Crown Publishers, Inc.
by arrangement with McGraw Hill Book Company, Inc.

C D E F G H

PRINTED IN THE UNITED STATES OF AMERICA

*This book is dedicated to my father*
DR. J. B. CLYMER

FOR MANY YEARS a small-town physician and surgeon, who never wavered in his belief that the automobile was destined to change the transportation system of the world. Dad, like many another doctor, was a pioneer in the use of the motorcar. Without top or windshield he drove the early cars through rain or snow, day or night, winter and summer, over rough dirt roads, whenever and wherever his services were needed. Financial remuneration was secondary, as he ministered to the rich, the poor, and the needy alike.

To him I owe all of the credit for whatever education and knowledge of early-day automobiles that I have acquired. He gave to me as a youngster the priceless opportunity of learning the fundamentals of design and construction by actual experience, which could be had only by ownership and association with the early-day automobiles that were the predecessors of the cars of today and of the future.

# PREFACE

THIS BOOK is meant to be neither an analytical study nor a definitive history of the American automobile. It is rather an album of automobile memories assembled by one who has bought, sold, collected, restored, raced, and even invented accessories for the American automobile. The author happened to be born about the time that Henry Ford was making his first experiments in a small workshop behind his house in Detroit and he has grown up with a generation that watched the Merry Oldsmobile and the Tin Lizzie make great changes in the American way of life. The automobile has added greater scope and dimension to the lives of every American; it has contributed new techniques and methods to American industry; it has inspired hundreds of songs, thousands of slogans, billions of dollars in advertising. It is too big a subject for one volume, even a series of volumes. *Treasury of Early American Automobiles*, therefore, means only to recall the glorious pioneer days of America's greatest industry.

# ACKNOWLEDGMENTS

In COMPILING a book such as *Treasury of Early American Automobiles* it becomes necessary to secure material from sources outside my own library. I therefore wish to thank the following persons and firms for their kind cooperation and assistance in supplying portions of the material included in this book:

General Motors Corporation, The Ford News Bureau, Chrysler Corporation, Hudson Motor Car Company, Packard Motor Car Company, The Studebaker Corporation, Reo Motors, The White Company, Nash-Kelvinator Corporation, International Harvester Company, Willys-Overland Company, Firestone Tire and Rubber Company, J. Frank Duryea, M. J. Duryea, Raymond W. Stanley, Carlton F. Stanley, Charles W. King, Ransom E. Olds, Earle C. Anthony, Thomas W. Galey, James Melton, Albert Mecham, Smith Hempstone Oliver, Peter Helck, Hi Sibley, W. Everett Miller, R. E. Anderson, Art Twohy, C. F. Greiner, Chet Ricker, Major Lennox R. Lohr, Harlan Appelquist, Ned Jordan, Joseph A. Stone, A. J. Arnheim.

# FOREWORD

IT IS with genuine pleasure that I write the foreword for Floyd Clymer's new book, *Treasury of Early American Automobiles*. As the reader looks back into what has been called "the good old days" he will be reminded of many pleasant memories, and probably a few memories of "get out and get under."

The author, Floyd Clymer, has paid many compliments to the pioneers who, by trial and error, perfected the basic mechanics of the automobile so that we, the motoring public, might have finer, safer and genuinely better motorcars. The position that the United States holds today as a leader of the automotive industry is, in reality, a tribute to these designers and builders of those early days.

It has given me a great deal of personal pleasure and satisfaction to collect some of the interesting early automobiles, and to restore and preserve them so that future generations might see the developments and progress made through the years, and possibly because of this, better appreciate the comforts that modern motoring affords.

This book illustrates and describes hundreds of the outstanding cars of yesteryear, as well as many of the lesser known makes. Besides being a memorial to the pioneer designers it is, I feel, a tribute to the workmen operating under a system of free enterprise and competition which in turn makes it possible for us all to drive better automobiles.

I want to give full credit to Floyd Clymer, whose persistent interest in a hobby in which he has indulged since boyhood has made available for all of us a phase of genuine American history that might otherwise have been lost. His efforts have also stimulated the restoration and operation of a great number of antique automobiles throughout the United States—these too might otherwise have been destroyed.

I think that *Treasury of Early American Automobiles* is a grand book, colorful and entertaining, and I am sure that the reader will get many hours of enjoyment from it. I feel that it fills a need for a good book on one of the most important phases of America's growth and development, and its pioneers are Americans who will be admired and remembered in days to come.

JAMES MELTON

# Treasury of
# Early American
# Automobiles

—·⊶✦⊷·—

## 1877 = 1925

THE most popular topic of conversation in America today, save perhaps the weather and the high cost of living, is the automobile. Fifty years ago, at the turn of the century, the automobile was as strange an apparition as the bearded lady in the circus. Barnum and Bailey, in 1896, gave the "famous Duryea motor-wagon" (page 4) top billing over the giant, the fat lady, and the albino. The horseless carriage seemed much more incredible to our grandfathers than a 6:35 express to the moon seems to us today. Besides, these chugging, clanking, hissing monsters frightened horses. Some early car enthusiasts were forced to take their machines apart and hide them in the woods at the approach of a horse and buggy. One state tried to pass a law that would have forced motorists to stop every ten minutes and shoot off Roman candles.

But the automobile survived. "Get a horse!" is not a cry one is apt to hear on Route 66 in the mid-twentieth century. Shown below is one of the very earliest horseless carriages, invented by George B. Selden (insert) in 1877. Its internal-combustion engine was mounted on the front axle, and by turning the wheels halfway around the motion of the car could be reversed. Although the date reads 1877, the car below was built in 1905-6, at which time Selden tried, unsuccessfully, to prove the practicality of his earlier invention in order to uphold his patent and keep competitors out of the field.

1

## Gas and Steam Power

In 1895, the year William Jennings Bryan started his "free silver" crusade, pioneer inventors were just as interested in steam and electric engines as they were in gasoline. One of the main drawbacks of the steam engine was the time it took to get the water hot. And then the steam boiler had a habit of blowing up in its owner's lap. Most of us remember the electric as something for Grandma to drive—slow and easy. When the emphasis was placed on speed, the electric car began to lose ground. The steam car still has its advocates, however. There are those who contend that, had men like Henry Ford turned their talents to the development of the steam car instead of the gasoline engine, our sleek, low-slung models would be carrying steam boilers under their long, shiny hoods today.

One of the very earliest steam cars, which looked suspiciously like the wedding of a buggy and a potbellied stove (top, left), was built by a Dr. J. W. Carhart in Racine, Wisconsin, in 1871. Ransom E. Olds of Lansing, Michigan, invented a steam carriage (left, middle) with a boiler, a gas tank, and a water tank. This vehicle with the fringe on top ran 15 miles on a filling of water and 40 on the gasoline that fired the boiler. According to the *Scientific American* of May 21, 1892, Mr. Olds stated that "it never kicks or bites, never tires on long runs, and never sweats in hot weather. It does not require care in the stable and only eats while on the road." Mr. Olds seemed to be implying that gasoline, in the good old days, was cheaper than hay.

The automobile on the lower left is the original Mueller-Benz car as it appeared in 1895 after placing second in the earliest recorded auto race.

Americans remember the turn of the century in terms of Dewey at Manila Bay and his famous order to the captain of the *Olympia*, "You may fire when ready, Gridley." No one begrudges the admiral his immortality, but humbler men—the Duryea brothers for instance—made even more spectacular contributions to American life and remain more or less unheralded by our history books. Charles and Frank Duryea built their first car in 1892, which, according to the advertisements, "actually operated under its own propulsion." A Duryea car won the first automobile race held in America, on Thanksgiving Day, 1895, from Chicago to Evanston, Illinois, and return. The start of that race is pictured below. The average speed was 5.05 miles per hour for the 52-mile run. One driver in the race had to drop out from sheer exhaustion.

The Smithsonian Institution now exhibits the 1893 Duryea (right, middle) and recognizes it as the "first marketable automobile in America." At the top, Charles Duryea—he was the super-salesman with the idea while his brother Frank was the mechanic—sits behind the steering lever of the 1895 Duryea.

# A Car at the Circus

Charles (right) and J. Frank Duryea (below) built the first marketable automobile in America. It made its premier appearance in Springfield, Massachusetts, in 1892. Left is the Duryea factory in Springfield, 1896. Note the rough facsimile of an assembly line. Below Barnum and Bailey advertise their strangest attraction—the horseless carriage.

Today, the great thundering automobile town in the United States is Detroit, Michigan. In 1896, a gasoline engine manufacturer by the name of Charles B. King drove the first automobile ever seen on the streets of Detroit. Mr. King is the man in the straw hat, one hand on the steering lever and the other on the brake (middle, right). King's first car, designed two years before in 1893 (bottom, right), had a steering wheel instead of a lever, left-hand drive, and a single-cylinder engine.

Another early automobile inventor was Elwood Haynes of Kokomo, Indiana (top, right), who later on somewhat erroneously called his machine "America's first car." Haynes built the car with the bicycle wheels in 1894 and went on to form his own company. Finally he joined the Apperson brothers, and together they manufactured the famous Haynes-Apperson.

It is hard for us to imagine the terror these motorized horse buggies struck into the hearts of the solid citizens of the 1890s. They shook and trembled and rattled and clattered. They spat oil, fire, smoke, and smell, and, to a person who disliked greasy machinery and had been brought up to expect the shiny elegance and perfection of the horse carriage, they were revolting.

The automobile has not always been the perfect specimen we see in the showrooms today. It muddled through by trial and error, and literally thousands of makes died along the way. It is a wonder that the industry ever survived such cars as The Seven Little Buffaloes, Autobug, Black Crow, Blood, Crusader, Darling, Eagle, Foos, Fish, Gyroscope, House, Duck, Klink, Leach, Moon, Sun, Star, Pet, Peter Pan, People's, Poppy, Vim, Viking, and some two thousand others.

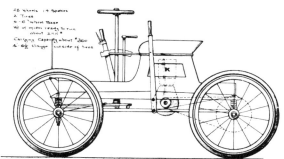

5

The automobile was no longer a circus oddity but was a relatively accepted vehicle by the time Henry Ford caught America's fancy in 1908 with the Model T, "The Universal Car." Here are three more very early models, all of which in one way or another contributed to Ford's ultimate success. In 1905 Elmer F. Lovejoy of Laramie, Wyoming, manufactured a car (top, left) with 4½-inch single-tube balloon tires. (In 1910, the author, at the age of fourteen, visited Mr. Lovejoy at his garage in Laramie.) Balloon tires were used as early as 1895 on the glorified three-wheel motocycle (middle, left) called the Pennington Victoria. The Victoria was another car produced in Racine, Wisconsin, an early center of automobile manufacturing. It was powered by two independently mounted 4¾-horsepower engines that were attached directly above the rear wheels.

J. W. Lambert of Anderson, Indiana, who built the Buckeye Gasoline Buggy (bottom, left), is also considered one of the early inventors of the automobile, and some even contend that he was the first. This fragile structure with the high wheels and the fringed top piece appears today as if it would come off a bad second in any encounter with a horse-drawn vehicle.

The high wheels on Lambert's and other early cars were necessary to negotiate the bumpy, high-center country roads of the 1890s. Modern cars, with their low streamlined bodies, would have had difficulty clearing the rocks and ruts in early roads.

Some early auto inventors thought springs might provide the power. D. I. Lybe of Sidney, Iowa, invented a spring bicycle (top, left) which he said would store up power while going downhill. A. B. Andrews of Center Point, Iowa, patented a 6-horsepower spring motor which he first attached to a baby carriage (middle, left). While going downhill, this mechanism also wound itself. The sketch at the bottom, left, is for a motor sleigh designed by R. H. Plass of Brooklyn. The Wing Work Wagon (top, right) is a forerunner of modern trucks, although L. J. Wing furnished only motors and connections to wagon manufacturers. Their motor made its own fuel from naphtha. Beneath the Wing truck are the De La Vergne "hunting trap" (right, middle) and Hill's Locomotor (right, bottom).

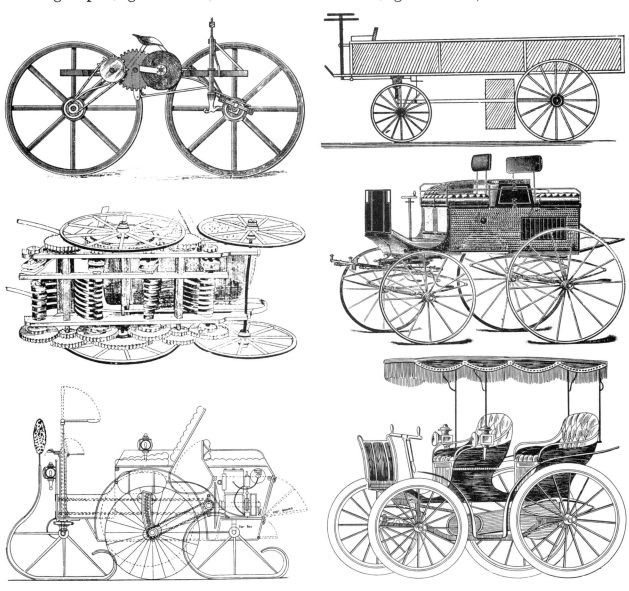

# Clippings from HORSELESS AGE Magazine

HORSELESS AGE was an early automobile magazine. The sketches below are from an 1895 copy: left, reading down, Salisbury Motocycle, Stewart Business Wagon, Holmes Gasoline Tricycle; right, Lewis Motocycle, Elston Gasoline Vehicle, Schoening Kerosene Carriage.

Most of these odd machines, from *Horseless Age* (1895), probably never got out of the blueprint stage, and certainly none of them withstood the test of time. Yet they all contributed to the final product: top left, the Burdick Spring Motor, in which you could use any number of springs according to the power desired; left middle, the Sweany Steam Carriage with four 3-horsepower motors, one attached to each wheel; top right, the Twombly Ether Bicycle; right middle, the Lawson 4-horsepower kerosene wagon motor; and, bottom, the Vanell Steam Carriage, which had a rotary motor attached to the driving shaft without gearing.

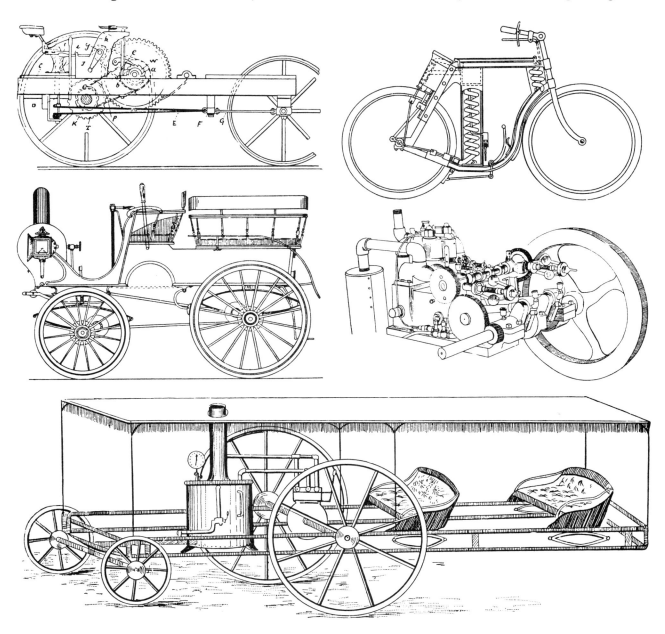

## First Oldsmobile, 1897

Ransom E. Olds, an automobile pioneer who had two cars named after him—the Oldsmobile and the Reo—was appointed manager of the Olds Motor Vehicle Company in 1897 (left). Its first model (left), completed that same year, is now in the Smithsonian Institution. Below is the shop in Lansing, Michigan, where the first Oldsmobile was built. As early as 1901, this automotive pioneer moved to Detroit and started to produce the famous curved-dash Oldsmobile. The Detroit factory burned and the company returned to Lansing. On page 11 there is a small Olds truck (top, left), a rather stuffy advertisement, and an early Oldsmobile price list. The "vapor" cars on this list were gasoline-powered. The prices are high but a few months later Olds produced the curved-dash model at $650, the first car to be mass produced.

## WE OFFER

N AN AUTOMOBILE OUR 15 YEARS EXPERIENCE as extensive manufacturers of the celebrated Olds Gasoline Engines and Motors, and therefore feel safe in assuring you that it has no equal. It starts at will by simply opening the throttle; its carriage body is free from machinery of any kind, which dispenses with all dirt or grease in the body, to say nothing of the inconvenience of getting at the machinery. Think of a motor that forms its own air-tight case, all parts inside, and every part mechanically oiled from one oil well, without the use of even an oil cup. It automatically regulates its speed; changes its spark for a high or low speed; throws out its compression for starting when stopping, and last but not least, throws in the auxiliary motor when excess power or speed is needed, or in case of an accident to the working cylinder the other cylinder throws in without any action on the part of the operator; in short, the **Olds** Motor Motes. Can never be appreciated until seen or tried. All of our **Vapor** Vehicles have 9 H.P. motors; wheels 34 and 36 inch, and pneumatic or cushion tires; speed 3 to 20 miles per hour; weight 1200 pounds.

Our Electric Vehicles are as good as any first-class storage battery carriage, and are mounted on the same running gear as the Vapor Automobiles.

**OLDS MOTOR WORKS, Detroit.**

## Oldsmobile Price List

TWO OR FOUR PASSENGER TRAP.

9 H. P. VAPOR MOTOR.

| | | | | |
|---|---|---|---|---|
| Runabout (vapor) | : | : | : | $1,000 |
| Delivery Wagon (vapor) | : | : | : | 1,200 |
| Trap, 2 or 4 passengers (vapor) | : | : | 1,200 |
| Stanhope (vapor) | : | : | : | 1,500 |
| Stanhope (electric) | : | : | : | 1,650 |
| Phaeton (vapor) | : | : | : | 1,600 |
| Phaeton (electric) | : | : | : | 1,750 |
| Cabriolet, 4 passengers (vapor) | : | : | 2,000 |
| Brougham, 2 passengers (vapor) | : | : | 2,000 |
| Brougham, 4 passengers (vapor) | : | : | 2,750 |

Many claim that the Winton No. 1 (top, right) was the first automobile purchased in the United States, April 1, 1898. It is now in the Smithsonian. . . . A seventeen-year-old Los Angeles boy, Earle C. Anthony, built his own electric automobile in 1897 (second photo, right). . . . A Missouri blacksmith, J. J. Gillinger, invented this rig (third photo, right) with the machine attached to a surrey. . . . The Davidson-Duryea Semi-Armored Car, 1898 (bottom, right), mounted a Colt automatic gun with armor shield, but seems to offer as much protection as a glass house.

## Montgomery Ward's Two Cars

In 1898 Montgomery Ward had two electric horseless carriages (below) made to order to use as "advertising novelties"; cost, $3,000 each. In their catalogue the company explains that their business is "selling anything and everything to farmers, mechanics, and country people at wholesale prices." The two electric cars were merely for the purpose of calling attention to their business. "We are sending them to the smaller towns of the Union so that those who might otherwise never see a horseless carriage will have the opportunity. . . ."

Thus, even as shrewd a concern as Montgomery Ward considered the automobile, in 1898, something a man should take his children to see before the fad passed on.

A sure sign that automobiles were proving commercially profitable, and therefore were here to stay, was the advent of competitive advertising around 1900. The Porter Stanhope ad on page 13 coins one of the first of innumerable car slogans—"The Only Perfect Automobile." Today, car slogans like "Ask the Man Who Owns One" and "Watch the Fords Go By" have become more familiar than the words to the second stanza of our national anthem. This Porter Stanhope ad has its slogan, cut, superlatives, and itemized facts.

# The Only Perfect Automobile!

**THE PORTER**

**STANHOPE**

**Weight**
**only 550lbs.**

———

**Order Now**
**to Ensure**
**Early**
**Delivery**

**THE PORTER**

**STANHOPE**

**Price**

**$750.00**

**Has no Rival**
**in**
**Simplicity,**
**Design,**
**Construction**
**Economy.**

The **"Motor Age"** of Chicago thus describes the Perfect Automobile:

"A handsome, stylish vehicle which can be started instantly and without previous laborious or lengthy preparation, can be stopped promptly, can be run at any speed up to twenty-five miles an hour, can be perfectly controlled by any person without special training, can travel over rough streets and roads, can climb stiff grades, can, in short, do anything and everything that a horse or span of horses attached to a vehicle can do, and do it more satisfactory, do it at a fraction of the expense and at the same time have none of the inherent faults of the horse, and no new ones of its own at the present time." There are vehicles that combine some of these advantages, but none that combine them all except

**THE PORTER STANHOPE,**
**price $750.00.**

We make only one grade, and that the best, and the best only will be found satisfactory in the long run.

**THE PORTER STANHOPE**
**is the Perfect Automobile.**

It is handsome and elegant in its lines and conforms in design to the modern horse carriages.

Safe, simple and durable.

Boiler is absolutely non-explosive and water-feed automatic.

It is free from all complications in its mechanism, so that an engineer is not necessary in its use.

Fuel is cheap and obtainable everywhere.

It is noiseless and free from all odor and vibration.

The Burner (or engine fire) is of low draft and so protected from the air as to be unquenchable in all weathers.

It is controlled by one lever only, as in times of danger several levers are confusing. The methods of lighting the burner at first are so simple that anyone can do it quickly and in a manner that is not complicated.

**Before you buy an Automobile mention** } **Write Now!**
**this magazine and write to the**

## PORTER MOTOR CO.,

**950 Tremont Building,** • • • • **Boston, Mass.**

13

In 1900 hearty, blustering Teddy Roosevelt jumped from the Governor's Mansion in Albany to the White House as Vice-president, and a few months later the assassination of McKinley made him Chief Executive. . . . The first White Steamer was manufactured in 1900 in Cleveland. This was the bright era for the steam car. In the bottom photograph Teddy Roosevelt himself doffs his hat to the crowd while sitting in a White. . . . The Grout (top) was a four-passenger (steam) trap built in Orange, Massachusetts.

# THE PHELPS TRACTOR.
## ........ 1901 ........

One of the earliest pieces of farm machinery, the unique Phelps Tractor manufactured in 1901, was designed for many uses. The steam engine could be attached to a buggy, a surrey, a light spring wagon, or a cart. It was advertised as a tractor of "universal application." Its boiler, with automatic fuel and water feed, required no attention and would run half a day without refilling. The small steam engine delivered up to 10 horsepower and was capable of a speed of 20 miles per hour.

The driver controlled the tractor with the reins, the only remaining throwback to the horse-and-buggy days. Drawing in the reins cut the speed, stopped the tractor, and finally backed it up. Loosening the reins increased the speed, but if they were dropped altogether, the engine stopped instantly, preventing a possible runaway. The driver also steered with the reins just as if he were guiding a horse.

## Bringing in The Yule Log

# The Oldsmobile

No roads too rough or uneven for the Oldsmobile. Its strong construction and simple mechanism are built to undergo the most severe usage. Its easy, cushioned frame affords perfect comfort to its occupants at all times. Embodying the latest improvements that our long experience has suggested, the Oldsmobile is to-day, in all seasons and on all roads, "the best thing on wheels."

For stormy weather, the Oldsmobile can be fitted with a waterproof top and apron that provides perfect protection for the occupants and the operating lever.

Selling agencies in all the large cities, or write for full information to Department G.

OLDS MOTOR WORKS, Detroit, U.S.A.
Member of the Association of Licensed Automobile Manufacturers.

---

# TRY IT AND YOU WILL BUY IT~~

THE FRIEDMAN ROAD WAGON, point for point, is the equal of any gasoline Automobile sold in the U.S. for $1,200, and is the only machine equipped with a Double Cylinder Four Cycle Balanced Engine that retails for less than that amount.

They will climb any grade up to 30%, and develop any speed up to 30 miles per hour. Absolute and instantaneous control. Every engine guaranteed to develop six horse-power.

Our price this year $750.00.

Hung on platform springs front and rear.

**Friedman Automobile Company**
**3 East Van Buren Street**
**Chicago, Ill.**

---

Two ads on this page guarantee auto care for a year, and the third claims to build "the best thing on wheels." As more companies sprang up, advertising grew more competitive. The California Automobile Company (right) pointed out that "we sell our vehicles $100 to $300 cheaper than Eastern firms." The Oldsmobile Company stated: "You can pay more money . . . and get more . . . trouble and profanity. If you are anxious to experiment, don't send for our catalogue."

## WE BUILD
# AUTOMOBILES

### GASOLINE
### STEAM
### ELECTRIC

Automobiles are in demand. California will manufacture and sell thousands
If you want to know how to get one write for particulars.

We can sell our vehicles at from $100 to $300 cheaper than Eastern manufacturers, and our prices will range from $500 for Runabout, to $3,000, according to style, power and speed. Order in person, by mail or through Bank.

"A Stylish Little Runabout."

WHEN YOU BUY AN AUTOMOBILE OF US WE GUARANTEE The vehicle for one year. Our FACTORY, where the machine is made, is at your disposal for any repairs or breakage. These can be attended to without the troublesome delays necessarily encountered when dealing with Eastern firms.

California Automobile Co.,

OFFICE AND FACTORY:
346 McAllister St., San Francisco, Cal.

The somber young man in the 1902 Oldsmobile (top, left) became President Hoover's Secretary of Commerce. Roy D. Chapin started with Oldsmobile in 1900 as a photographer. In addition he spent several hours a day filing castings. In 1902 he made the first solo auto trip from Detroit to New York, in nine days. He almost met disaster on Fifth Avenue when the runabout skidded into the curb, damaging one of the wire wheels. At Chapin's hotel the doorman would not let him in because of the nine days' accumulation of mud and grease on his clothes, and the boy who was later to become the nation's Secretary of Commerce had to sneak in through the servants' entrance.

A Cornell student, Clarence W. Spicer, built a car in 1902 (middle, left) to try out universal joints and a propeller-shaft drive. Spicer developed universal joints, shafts, and axles for auto companies, and the result was the now famous Spicer Manufacturing Company of Toledo, makers of automobile parts.

T. M. Galey's 1902 Winton Surrey (left, bottom) was one of the earliest cars equipped with wheel steering and single-tube pneumatic tires.

17

# STEAM CARS

OF the thirty-four makes of cars exhibited in the first automobile show at Madison Square Garden in 1900, seven were steam cars. The vogue for steam lasted several years, and among the better known makes were the Stanley, the White, the Locomobile, the Lane, and the Doble. The steamer had certain advantages such as smooth operation, unexcelled power, and quick acceleration. It was almost impossible to stall a steamer if its rear wheels could secure traction. Disadvantages included the several minutes it required to get steamed up, the limited number of miles that could be traveled on one boilerful of water, the quick corrosion of the boiler, and the difficulties encountered with the burner.

The three-wheel steam car below—one of the first—was designed by L. D. Copeland in the early 1880s. It had a kerosene oil burner and a ½-horsepower single-cylinder engine.

## Five Early Steam Cars

In one of the earliest recorded auto races, in Hartford, Connecticut, in 1899, a Stanley Steamer, the odds-on favorite, lost out to a gas-powered Columbia in a 5-mile race because the Stanley ran out of steam. Hissing and quivering, the Stanley jumped into the lead and was half-way around the track before the Columbia could get into high gear. Despite the tremendous initial advantage, the steamer's speed tapered off as it used up its surplus steam pressure, and the little gas car—like the proverbial tortoise, slow but sure—took the lead as they headed into the stretch and won the race by one-eighth of a mile.

Top, left, is a steam car built by Ransom E. Olds, later of Oldsmobile and Reo fame, in 1886. Below are four steam cars of the turn of the century: top, left, a steam car built in 1900 by Carl Breer, later a Chrysler engineer; bottom, left, a 1903 Stanley Steamer that carried its passengers in front of and below the driver; top, right, the first White Steamer, built in 1900 and now on display in the Smithsonian Institution; bottom, right, the first truck built by the White Motor Company, 1901.

## Steam Cars Had Speed

Despite their belonging to antiquity, steamers are still to be admired for, among other things, their early speed records. In 1906 Fred Marriott (below, left) in a Stanley Steamer at Ormond Beach, Florida, established a world's record of 127 miles per hour that still stands today for cars having less than 30 horsepower.

In 1905 the steam car, at the height of its popularity, received official recognition to the extent of participating in a presidential inauguration. At top left, a White Steamer leads the 1905 inaugural parade for President Theodore Roosevelt. Below is a 1903 advertisement for a Jaxon Steam Car.

The Stanley Steamer was a popular and powerful car, and its rounded hood was for many years a distinguishing trademark. At right are two 1908 Stanleys. The two-seater, top right, went under the rather risqué name of "Gentlemen's Speedy Roadster" (no wonder Victorian mothers had qualms about their daughters' venturing out in horseless carriages!), while the more respectable family vehicle below was known as the "Touring Car."

Below, President William Howard Taft and family ride in a 1909 White Steamer. Seated directly in front of the President is his son, Robert, who later became a U.S. Senator.

# Facts about Steam Cars

 Steam cars were in use long before gasoline automobiles appeared on the scene.  The Stearns Steamer was built in Syracuse, New York, in 1889.  Webb Jay, renowned early-day racing driver, won many spectacular racing events in the famous White Steam Car Racer, "Whistling Billy."  Fred Marriott, in a Stanley Steamer, was the first human being to travel over 2 miles per minute when he established the world's speed record of 127 miles per hour at Ormond Beach, Florida, in 1906.  A car called the Delling had a three-cylinder steam engine.  The Stanley and Doble engines were mounted on the rear axle, while the White Steamer had the engine located under the hood.

## How Much Do You Remember about Steam Cars?

*(Answers are printed below)*

1. What steam car had the same name as a famous piano?
2. There were twelve makes of steam cars with the same names as cities in the United States. Can you name them?
3. What steam car had the same name as a judicial court?
4. What steam car had the name of a dwelling?
5. What steam car had the name of a president of the United States?
6. What steam car had the same name as a one-time Secretary of State?
7. What steam car had the same name as a member of a train crew?
8. What steam car had the same name as a famous brand of silverware?
9. What man who made two makes of gasoline cars built an experimental steam car in 1897?
10. What make of steam car had the same name as a famous maker of cheese?
11. What steam car had the same name as a contest winner?
12. What steam car had the name of a famous watch?
13. What steam car had the name of a famous sewing machine?

### ANSWERS TO QUESTIONS ABOVE

1. Baldwin. 2. Chicago, Malden, Mobile, Pawtucket, Reading, Toledo, Cincinnati, Milwaukee, Ormond, Prescott, Rochester, Waltham. 3. Federal. 4. House. 5. Johnson. 6. Kellogg. 7. Porter. 8. Rogers. 9. R. E. Olds (Olds and Reo). 10. Kraft. 11. Victor. 12. Waltham. 13. White.

# Steam Automobiles

At one time, steam cars were strong competition for gas cars. Here is a list of 124 makes of steam automobiles once manufactured in the United States. Of these not a single one is made today.

| | | | |
|---|---|---|---|
| American, 1900 | Eclipse | Leach | Simons |
| American, 1922 | Elberon | Locke | Skene |
| Artzberger | Elite | Locomobile | Spencer |
| Aultman | Empire | Loomis | Springer |
| Austin | Endurance | Lutz | Springfield |
| Auto-Loco | Essex | Lyons | Squier |
| Baker | Federal | Malden | Standard |
| Baldwin | Field | Mason | Stanley |
| Ball | Foster | McKay | Stanton |
| Best | Gaeth | Mercury | Steamobile |
| Binney-Burnham | Gearless | Meteor | Stearns |
| Boss | Geneva | Mills | Sterling |
| Brecht | Grout | Milwaukee | Stewart-Coats |
| Bristol | Hartley | Mobile | Storck |
| Cameron | Hess | Morse | Strathmore |
| Cannon | Hoffman | New England | Stringer |
| Capitol | Holland | Ormond | Strouse |
| Century | Holyoke | Overholt | Super-Steamer |
| Cincinnati | House | Overman | Taunton |
| Clark | Howard | Oxford | Terwilliger |
| Clermont | Hudson | Pawtucket | Thompson |
| Coats | International | Peerless | Toledo |
| Conrad | Jaxon | Porter | Tractmobile |
| Cotta | Johnson | Prescott | Trask-Detroit |
| Crompton | Keene | Puritan | Trinity |
| Crouch | Kellogg | Randolph | Victor |
| Delling | Kensington | Reading | Waltham |
| Detroit | Keystone | Remel-Vincent | Watt |
| Doble | Kidder | Rogers | Webb-Jay |
| Dudgeon | Kraft | Ross | Westfield |
| Eastman | Lane | Scott-Newcomb | White |

## Coast to Coast, 1903

AT the turn of the century, driving a car coast to coast was more difficult than swimming the English Channel is today. In 1903 Tom Fetch, in a single-cylinder Packard (top, left), backed his car's rear wheels into San Francisco Bay and then drove over mountains, deserts, and plains to New York City in 61 days. His car, affectionately dubbed "Old Pacific," is preserved today in the Greenfield Museum in Dearborn, Michigan.

Those formidable gentlemen behind the mustaches (left) are not Keystone cops, but fire fighters. Their Stanley Steamer is thought to be the first such vehicle used by a fire department. Newton, Massachusetts, was the forward-looking town, 1903 the date. Their main fire-fighting equipment seems to be a hand extinguisher. . . . Below, eight fashionable Denver ladies go sight-seeing in White Steamers, 1903.

In 1895 the automobile was practically unknown. Ten years later it was the product of a hundred-million-dollar business. In 1895 the factory was a barn with a drill press, a lathe, and a mechanic. Ten years later auto pioneers were faced with a public clamoring for their product. The cows were driven out of the barn, and assembly lines took their place.

The shrewd manufacturer outdid his competitor in new features, advertising stunts, and tricky slogans. Into the field came safety guards (the forerunners of bumpers), front guards, some of which resembled locomotive cowcatchers, and the tilting steering wheel "to aid stout people getting in and out of the driver's seat."

In 1903 Ford put out his first Model A, a two-cylinder job (top, right) which cranked on the side, had two speeds forward and one reverse, and was stylishly appointed with plush leather seats and gleaming metal headlights. "Polished brass rails" are advertised for the fashionable car (right, middle), and the $850 Fordmobile (right, bottom) boasts absolutely no "smell, noise, or jolt." Below are three more 1903 advertisements.

## Cadillac, Haynes, and Packard, 1903

Below are the 1903 models of three famous cars, two of which are still in existence today, a half century later: a one-cylinder Cadillac (top, left) with a water-cooled engine, a bulb horn on the steering column, and two kerosene headlamps; a Haynes-Apperson that "won every endurance contest in the United States and every contest or race it ever entered"; and an early Packard automobile (with a cyclops-like headlight) using the slogan so well known today, "Ask the Man Who Owns One."

### The Only One That Always Won
## The HAYNES-APPERSON

WON EVERY ENDURANCE CONTEST HELD IN AMERICA, EVERY CONTEST OR RACE EVER ENTERED, MORE RECORDS THAN ANY OTHER MADE IN THE UNITED STATES, and was the only gasolene car that ran the contest from New York to Boston and back without repairs or adjustments OF ANY KIND. . . . . . . .

**Phaeton
12 h. p.
$1500**

No other combines any two of these features: Double opposed-cylinder motor (originated by us—widely copied). Four-speed transmission controlled by the simple motion of a single lever. Adjustable steering wheel. The only *positive* carburetors on earth. *Safe* steering pivots. Luxurious ease of riding.

Surrey, $1800. Runabout, $1200. *Tonneau ready by spring.*
Inquirers are urged to visit our factory, where every detail of Haynes-Apperson Superiority can be seen and fully understood.

**HAYNES-APPERSON CO., - - Kokomo, Ind., U. S. A.**
*The oldest makers of motor cars in America*
**Branch Store, 381 to 385 Wabash Ave., Chicago**
Eastern Representatives
Brooklyn Automobile Co., 1239-41-43 Fulton St., Brooklyn, N. Y.
*New York Location To Be Announced*
National Automobile & Mfg. Co., Pacific Coast Agents, San Francisco.

*Packard*
## MOTOR CAR

has been made famous simply by what it does. Its perfect performance in every public contest has, of course, had much to do with its splendid reputation as a reliable touring car, but it is the unbroken line of satisfied users who are responsible for its great popularity. Write for catalogue about the Packard Motor Car and

### "ASK THE MAN WHO OWNS ONE"
## Packard Motor Car Co.
### WARREN, OHIO

New York, Geo. B. Adams, Mgr., 317 W. 59th St.
Philadelphia, Wm. Rudolph, 302 N. Broad St.
Boston, H. B. Shattuck & Son, 239 Columbus Ave.
Chicago, Pardee & Co., 1401 Michigan Boulevard.
Los Angeles, Norman W. Church, 439 S. Main St.
San Francisco, H. B. Larzalere, 1814 Market St.

In 1879 George B. Selden, whose pioneer horseless carriage is pictured on page 1, applied for a patent which seemed to cover any self-propelled gasoline-powered vehicle. For years most American automobile manufacturers honored this patent and paid royalties to the Association of Licensed Automobile Manufacturers which controlled the Selden Patent. It was common practice for the Association to warn and threaten automobile makers and users not licensed under the Selden Patent that they would be prosecuted.

One of the first automobile manufacturers to contest the validity of the Selden Patent was Henry Ford. In many early advertisements (below), sometimes printed side by side, Ford would personally guarantee protection to every Ford dealer and Ford owner against damages resulting from any patent suit, while the Association of Licensed Automobile Manufacturers charged that "no other manufacturers or importers (except those working under the Selden Patent) are authorized to make or sell gasoline automobiles."

Ford's spirited and persistent defense in the Selden Patent suit saved the automobile industry a great deal of trouble. A decision against Ford and upholding the Patent was reached in 1909, but in 1911 the decision was reversed in a Court of Appeals.

## NOTICE

To Manufacturers, Dealers, Importers, Agents and Users of

## Gasoline Automobiles

United States Letters Patent No. 549,160, granted to George B. Selden, November 5th, 1895, controls broadly all gasoline automobiles which are accepted as commercially practical. Licenses under this patent have been secured from the owners by the following named manufacturers and importers

| | |
|---|---|
| Electric Vehicle Co. | Pope Motor Car Co. |
| The Winton Motor Carriage Co. | The J. Stevens Arms and Tool Co. |
| Packard Motor Car Co. | H. H. Franklin Mfg. Co. |
| Olds Motor Works. | Charron, Giradot & Voigt |
| Knox Automobile Co. | Company of America. |
| The Haynes-Apperson Co. | (Smith & Mabley) |
| The Autocar Co. | The Commerial Motor Co. |
| The George N. Pierce Co. | Berg Automobile Co. |
| Apperson Bros. Automobile Co. | Cadillac Automobile Co. |
| Searchmont Automobile Co. | Northern Manufacturing Co. |
| Locomobile Company of America. | Pope-Robinson Co. |
| The Peerless Motor Car Co. | The Kirk Manufacturing Co. |
| U S Long Distance Auto. Co. | Elmore Mfg. Co. |
| Waltham Manufacturing Co. | E. R. Thomas Motor Co. |
| Buffalo Gasolene Motor Co. | The F. B. Stearns Company. |

These manufacturers are pioneers in this industry, and have commercialized the gasoline vehicle by many years of development, and at a great cost. They are the owners of upwards of four hundred United States Patents, covering many of the most important improvements and details of manufacture. Both the basic Selden patent and all other patents owned as aforesaid will be enforced against all infringers

No other manufacturers or importers are authorized to make or sell gasoline automobiles, and any person making, selling or using such machines made or sold by any unlicensed manufacturers or importers will be liable to prosecution for infringement.

## Association of Licensed Automobile Manufacturers

No. 7 EAST 42nd STREET, NEW YORK

## NOTICE

To Dealers, Importers, Agents and Users of Our

## Gasoline Automobiles

WE will protect you against any prosecution for alleged infringements of patents. Regarding alleged infringement of the Selden patent we beg to quote the well-known Patent Attorneys, Messrs. Parker and Burton: "The Selden patent is not a broad one, and if it was it is anticipated. It does not cover a practicable machine, no practicable machine can be made from it and never was so far as we can ascertain. It relates to that form of carriage called a FORE CARRIAGE. None of that type has ever been in use, all have been failures. No court in the United States has ever decided in favor of the patent on the merits of the case, all it has ever done was to record a prior agreement between parties."

We are pioneers of the GASOLINE AUTOMOBILE. Our Mr. Ford made the first Gasoline Automobile in Detroit and the third in the United States. His machine made in 1893 (two years previous to the granting of the Selden patent, Nov. 5, 1895) is still in use. Our Mr. Ford also built the famous "999" Gasoline Automobile, which was driven by Barney Oldfield in New York on July 25th, 1903, a mile in 55 4-5 seconds on a circular track, which is the world's record.

Mr. Ford, driving his own machine, beat Mr. Winton at Grosse Pointe track in 1901. We have always been winners

*Write for Catalogue.*

## FORD MOTOR COMPANY

688-692 Mack Avenue, - - - DETROIT, MICH.

## The Water-Gasoline Car, 1903

In 1903 James A. Charter invented a car that threatened to solve all and any gasoline shortages. The Charter Water-Gasoline car (two photographs, left) operated on a combination of water and gasoline. The gasoline vapor and the atomized water were sucked by the piston into the cylinder at the same time. There was about half as much water as there was gasoline in each charge. The effect claimed was that when the "charge," as they called it, reached the heated cylinder, the water was quickly converted into superheated steam. Note also the folding seats, which permitted immediate access to the engine. The Charter automobile needed no temperature gauge because of the convenient position of the engine under the front seats. As soon as it got too hot to sit down, you knew your automobile was running a high fever. The Charter water-gasoline theory was one of the saner unsuccessful methods that our early inventors considered for powering the horseless carriage. Kerosene, springs, compressed air, and gravity were all considered at one time or another.

Below, the old *Life* magazine has some fun at the expense of the early car owner, 1903.

"How quickly could you stop if necessary?"

"About like that."

Early car manufacturers found it difficult to separate the idea of the horseless carriage from the horse and carriage, as in the cartoon at the right. Early automobiles had carriage wheels, a carriage dashboard, carriage springs, and sometimes even reins instead of a steering wheel. To preserve the time-honored shape of the buggy, the engine was hidden beneath and to the rear. One Uriah Smith actually employed a horse's head (below).

When the automobile industry was young, auto racing was an important element in advertising. The big companies built special racing cars and hired daredevil drivers to race them. Barney Oldfield (bottom, left, in the Winton Bullet No. 2) first became famous as an automobile racer when he drove the famous Ford "999." Until 1912 Barney Oldfield appeared at state and country fairs, exhibitions, and leading race tracks everywhere, winning many of the important races in the United States. The traffic cops of the day, instead of asking, "Where ya going, to a fire?" would say to the offending motorist, "Who do you think you are, Barney Oldfield?" Youngsters all over the country idolized Oldfield, and his familiar signature, "You know me, Barney Oldfield," and his ever-present cigar became famous trade-marks.

Alexander Winton (left, middle) poses in 1903 with his Winton Bullet No. 2.

29

# CADILLAC — A $900 TOURING CAR

The single cylinder Cadillac was one of the few early day cars that cranked on the opposite side from most of the "side-winders." The crank was detachable.

The hole where the starting crank was inserted can be seen in the illustration, directly back of the front fender and below the seat.

## THE AUTOMOBILE ALL MAKERS HOPE SOME DAY TO EQUAL.

There is no Automobile the equal of the CADILLAC
at the price of a CADILLAC.

CADILLAC AUTOMOBILE COMPANY, DETROIT, MICH.

Member of Association of Licensed Automobile Manufacturers.

Zip! went the spark
On flew the Knox
Were never folks so
glad

There Are Two Classes of Air Cooling Systems for
Automobile Car Cylinders—

# KNOX AND OTHERS

WHAT the others *try* to do the Knox *does*. That's the practical difference. Some keep cool *part* of the time. The Knox keeps cool *all* of the time. And it does it *automatically!* No wonder the Knox is known as

## "The Car That Obviates the Tow"

NOTE—The Knox Patent System of automatic air cooling consists of corrugated pins on the exterior of the cylinder in connection with an air blast produced by a fan. The corrugated pins surrounding the cylinder are two inches in length, and are screwed into the surface of each cylinder.

### They Radiate the Heat!

and make it possible to obtain 32 square inches of heat radiating surface per square inch of outside surface of cylinder surface. This is about four and one-half times that obtainable with the ordinary type of air cooled cylinder with cast flanges. Knox Waterless Gasoline Engines do not overheat in summer.

SELLING AGENCIES IN ALL PRINCIPAL CITIES

## KNOX AUTOMOBILE COMPANY
### Springfield, Mass.

Members of Association of Licensed Automobile Manufacturers.

A $900 Cadillac, a remnant of the good old days of 1904, is advertised on the left. Below it, the now defunct Knox Automobile Company advertises its spark plugs (which work with "Zip!") and its automatic air cooling with its Waterless Gasoline Engine.

In 1904 the automobile seems to have been confused with the railroad. Mr. and Mrs. Charles Glidden (below), sponsors of the famous Glidden Tours, are shown arriving at Vancouver, British Columbia, after a 3,536-mile trip from Boston. This car, a Napier, was the first automobile to cross the Canadian Rockies; 1,733 miles were traveled on roads, and 1,803 miles on railroad tracks for which special flanged wheels were used. The car was dispatched as a special train and provided with a conductor, torpedoes, and red flags.

Twenty years ago people did not have the vaguest idea of the ultimate form of the automobile. Perhaps the same thing can be said of car designers today. While yesterday cars were high and narrow, today they are low and wide; but that does not mean the trend can't change. Recently there have been complaints that most new cars on a bumpy country road do not have enough clearance. It is also said by some that the width of modern cars makes it difficult to park on city streets and that the driver's visibility is not what it used to be, even though more glass is used.

On this page are pictured some car ideas that were brand new in 1904. Top, right, we have an Oldsmobile Railroad Inspection Car priced at $450. Bottom, left, is a compressed-air truck built by the American Wheelock Engine Company of Worcester, Massachusetts. The air was delivered from high-pressure steel bottles. The Model L Rambler (bottom, right) featured a canopy top with long flowing drapes. Dr. Dyke's book on the *Diseases of Gasoline Automobiles and How to Remedy Them* (top, left) looks today as if it probably was a joke in 1904, but the odds are that Dr. Dyke was in deadly earnest.

DR. DYKES "Diseases of Gasolene Automobiles and How to Remedy Them."
PRICE $1.50. A book worth the money.
Send 10 cents for largest Automobile Supply Catalogue in the World.
A. L. Dyke Automobile Supply Co.
2108 OLIVE STREET,    ST. LOUIS, MO.

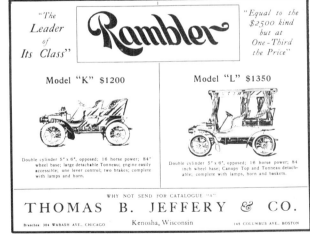

"The Leader of Its Class"    **Rambler**    "Equal to the $2500 kind but at One-Third the Price"

Model "K" $1200

Double cylinder 5" x 6", opposed; 16 horse power; 84" wheel base; large detachable Tonneau; engine easily accessible; one lever control; two brakes; complete with lamps and horn.

Model "L" $1350

Double cylinder 5" x 6", opposed; 16 horse power; 84 inch wheel base; Canopy Top and Tonneau detachable; complete with lamps, horn and baskets.

WHY NOT SEND FOR CATALOGUE "A"
THOMAS   B.   JEFFERY   &   CO.
Branches: 304 WABASH AVE, CHICAGO    Kenosha, Wisconsin    145 COLUMBUS AVE, BOSTON

## Buick, Olds, and Ford, 1904

In 1904 Theodore Roosevelt won an overwhelming victory at the polls over Judge Alton B. Parker. The President's attempt to enforce the Sherman Antitrust Act against monopolistic concerns in no way affected the infant automobile industry, although two great automobile names of today—Ford and Buick—began to manufacture, in 1903 and 1904, the first of a long line of famous cars. Ransom E. Olds's curved-dash Oldsmobile, David Buick's Model B (now General Motors), and Henry Ford's Model B were all being produced at that time.

The cars of those three pioneers, and the 1904 Pierce Great-Arrow, are pictured on this page. The Pierce Great-Arrow's gearshift lever (top, left) was on the steering column, as in many early models, in exactly the same place modern cars have their gearshifts today.

The generator on the side of the car was for the gas lamps, and the trap door under the front seat was for tools. Passengers entered the rear seat by a rear door in the tonneau.

The curved-dash Oldsmobile (at the left, middle) still adhered to the principle of the steering tiller, seated two persons, and sold for only $650. Its official title was the "Oldsmobile Regular Runabout" and its gasoline capacity was only five gallons.

The Model B Ford (bottom, left) was manufactured from 1904 to 1906. It was Ford's first four-cylinder model and also the first Ford engine to be located under the hood. It had copper water jackets. It sold for $2,000.

The 1904 Buick Model B (bottom, right) was built in Jackson, Michigan, and the total year's production was 37. This car sold for $850.

Three turn-of-the-century advertisements accentuate the passing of the years. Columbia Automobiles (top, left) offer everything from Tonneaus, Cabriolets, Surreys, and Broughams to Police Patrols and Ambulances. The Roadster (bottom) stands "ace high" (a vague sort of recommendation) and advertises a "muffler that muffles" and eighteen coats of paint. "She's a great favorite with the physicians." Ham's Auto Inspector-and-Tail Lamp has a "ruby lens" and guarantees to light with "just one match."

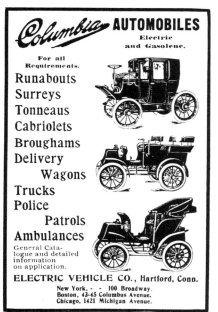

*Columbia* **AUTOMOBILES**
**Electric and Gasolene.**

**For all Requirements.**

Runabouts
Surreys
Tonneaus
Cabriolets
Broughams
Delivery
    Wagons
Trucks
Police
    Patrols
Ambulances

General Catalogue and detailed information on application.

**ELECTRIC VEHICLE CO., Hartford, Conn.**

New York, - - 100 Broadway.
Boston, 43-45 Columbus Avenue.
Chicago, 1421 Michigan Avenue.

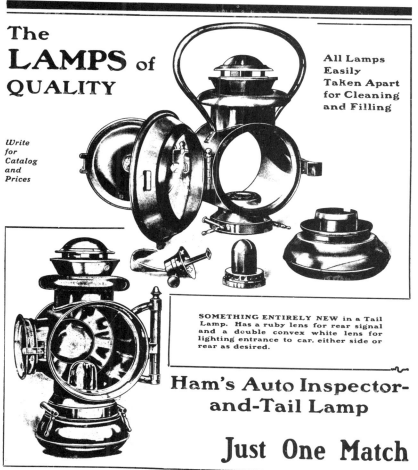

The **LAMPS** of **QUALITY**

All Lamps Easily Taken Apart for Cleaning and Filling

*Write for Catalog and Prices*

SOMETHING ENTIRELY NEW in a Tail Lamp. Has a ruby lens for rear signal and a double convex white lens for lighting entrance to car, either side or rear as desired.

**Ham's Auto Inspector-and-Tail Lamp**

**Just One Match**

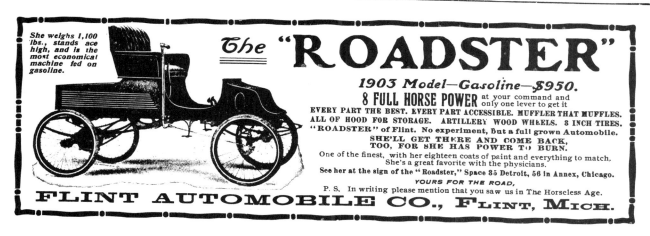

She weighs 1,100 lbs., stands ace high, and is the most economical machine fed on gasoline.

*The* **"ROADSTER"**

*1903 Model—Gasoline—$950.*

**8 FULL HORSE POWER** at your command and only one lever to get it

EVERY PART THE BEST. EVERY PART ACCESSIBLE. MUFFLER THAT MUFFLES. ALL OF HOOD FOR STORAGE. ARTILLERY WOOD WHEELS. 3 INCH TIRES. "ROADSTER" of Flint. No experiment, But a full grown Automobile.

**SHE'LL GET THERE AND COME BACK, TOO, FOR SHE HAS POWER TO BURN.**

One of the finest, with her eighteen coats of paint and everything to match. She's a great favorite with the physicians.

See her at the sign of the "Roadster," Space 35 Detroit, 56 in Annex, Chicago.

*YOURS FOR THE ROAD,*

P. S.  In writing please mention that you saw us in The Horseless Age.

**FLINT AUTOMOBILE CO., FLINT, MICH.**

# Their First Car

She Wants It

He Gets It

To the Country

34

*Pass a Farmer*

*Scare the Horse*

*Break Down*

*Farmer Comes*

*Happy Ending*

35

COMPANIES that manufactured only twenty cars a year mushroomed all over America around 1905. Some advertised gasoline, steam, or electric models. Others offered car bodies built to order. The methods of production were simple but wasteful of human energy. A group of three or four men huddled around a frame, adding parts that they had hauled in trucks from other sections of the factory.

Here are advertisements for three 1905 models long since extinct and a photograph of a two-cylinder 1905 Overland (later the Willys Overland).

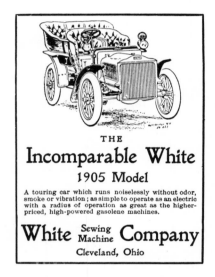

Unlike modern motorists, the automobile pioneers in 1905 had to be interested in the component parts—like spark plugs (right)—of their automobiles. Much of the repair work was done at home and by the owner.

Early owners will remember the Pope Motor Company (bottom, left) of Hartford. Many cars bore the Pope name: the Pope-Hartford, Pope-Tribune, Pope-Toledo, and others. The Ford Model F (bottom, right) came out in 1905.

# ELECTRIC CARS

FROM 1900 to 1915 at least 25 well-known electric-car companies advertised vehicles which were "clean, quiet, stylish, and easy to operate—the only car for a lady." The electric car was considered not only a mode of transportation but a social asset. The last electric-car company, the Detroit Electric, still made cars on special order in the 1930s. Electricity is used today to power invalid cars and certain types of commercial vehicles, such as delivery trucks and indoor factory cars. . . . Some of the earliest electric models are pictured below. Top, left, is the Baker and Elberg Electric Wagon. Bottom, left, is the Sturges Electric Motocycle, and top, right, the Barrows Electric Tricycle. The Dey Griswold Electric Phaeton (bottom, right) shows the refinements which made the later electric a social asset.

If the electric had advantages, it had more drawbacks. It would run only 40 to 60 miles before it became necessary to recharge the batteries. Some owners had a battery-charging unit in their own garage but most, particularly in the cities, placed their electrics in a garage for "live storage," and the service would include charging the batteries overnight. The popularity of the electric car began to wane about 1912 when gasoline cars became easier to operate and offered higher speed and a wider range of operation.

# FLANDERS COLONIAL ELECTRIC

THIS IS JUST TO SAY that we are now delivering Flanders Electrics as fast as we can and that the advent of this beautiful car itself on the streets of the various cities has created a sensation greater even than did its announcement through the press a few months ago.

OF COURSE PEOPLE ARE IMPATIENT for deliveries and dealers are berating us for not doing the impossible. We can't supply everybody at once—nor can we hope to deliver every car that is ordered on the day.

THAT'S THE BEST PART OF IT—the demand is four or five times the possible supply. No dealer likes to handle a line that is a drug on the market and no man or woman cares to buy a car that nobody else wants.

THAT'S THE BEST PROOF of quality—over-demand. Buyers know and they don't make mistakes unanimously. You can accept it as a rule that those cars which enjoy the greatest demand are the best cars.

"WELL ADVERTISED," YOU SAY—well perhaps. In fact we admit as much—howbeit reluctantly.

BUT THE AD STOPS at the point where it has created interest—induced inspection and trial of the article itself.

THAT'S WHY WE'RE SO PLEASED at the enthusiasm created by the advent on the streets of the Flanders Electric itself—it has more than justified every statement made in the ad.

BY THE WAY: The most striking and the most convincing evidence of the triumph of this car is seen in the shows this year—every live manufacturer—and even some of the half dead ones—has redesigned to meet the specifications of the Flanders low-hung, roomy, Colonial Electric Some of them imitate it fairly well in appearance and approximate it to some degree in silence and performance—at twice or three times the price.

DEALERS:—A few towns still open—if you want to get in on the agency for "the car that sells itself," better write today.

## FLANDERS MANUFACTURING COMPANY

The stylish lady's electric could not travel far unless its battery was recharged. The weight-power ratio was another problem to be considered; a light gasoline car could have as much power as a ponderous electric. Also, for every battery charge, the electric would develop approximately 15 horsepower-hours, and the gasoline car, for every tank of gas, would develop 40. Thus the operating radius of the gasoline type was almost thrice that of the electric.

Such ads as these introduced a new element into car advertising that has not disappeared to this day—snob appeal. The occupants of the Flanders Colonial Electric (left) are decked out in top hats and evening gowns while (below, left) the "Stately, Stylish Electric Stanhope . . . is the aristocrat of motors."

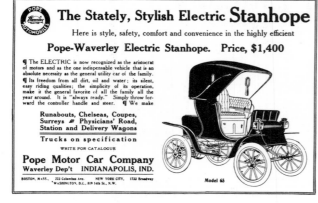
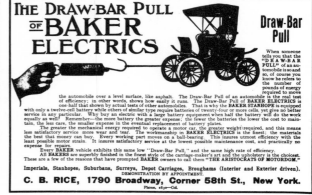

The fashionable lady under the parasol on the right is Mrs. Norman R. Hartley of Pittsburgh in her 1901 Columbia Electric. This shiny, spotless electric was the perfect vehicle of fashion—no crank to turn; no rumbles, rattles, or terrifying explosions; no gasoline fumes, oil, or grease. Mrs. Hartley undoubtedly descended from her electric as neat, trim, and well-pressed as she stepped in. . . . Below, the late C. P. Steinmetz, famous General Electric engineer, leans on the running board of a 1914 Detroit Electric. Despite the gleaming finish, the vaselike lamps, and the flower container, the electric could not compete with the gas car.

## The Personal Approach, 1905

In 1905 there was a "buyer's market" in the automobile trade and the car buyer had to be convinced. The letter (below) from dealer to buyer mentions a $750 Cadillac and "a machine called the Buick which is new to the automobile world this year." Even with a few spelling and typographical errors, these personal letters, and in general the initiative of the early salesmen and manufacturers, helped immensely in getting the idea of the horseless carriage across to a skeptical public. The 1905 *Life* magazine cartoon (below, right) reflects that skepticism.

H. E. PENCE,
President

THE LARGEST AUTOMOBILE HOUSE IN THE WEST

# PENCE AUTOMOBILE COMPANY

717-719 HENNEPIN AVENUE

PENCE AUTOMOBILE CO.,
Porritt Blk., 5th St. and N. P. Ave.,
FARGO, N. D.   Phone 148.

AUTOMOBILE DEPARTMENT

Fargo, N. D. April 22, 1905.

Mr. Lee Coombs,
   Valley City, N. D.

Dear Sirs:-

     We are informed that you are in the market this year for an automobile.  In two of our machine we have about all you can find in the market and are satisfied that they will fill your requirements.   The writer has visited your city a number of times and has used an automobile there and is well aware of the conditions under which you will have to use a machine.   The Cadillac tonneau car weighs 1500 lbs and with the power they are putting in it are satisfied that they are giving more for the money than you can get in any other machines.   The car with side door entrance sells for $950 and the runabout with the same engine and power but with smaller wheels and tires sells for $750.   The runabout is the highest powered runabout for its weight in the market.   We have a machine called the Buick which is new to the Automobile world this year which develops 22 h. p. nad with the finish they put on their bodies is the best high powerd proposition on the market.   It sells for $1200.   Would be very glad indeed to have you call and look over our machines and in case we have a machine that will suit you the writer will deliver the machine to you in such a way as to give you a thorough knowledge of the inside of the machine and we think save you some of the delays and inconveniences that the people of your city have had in the past.   Trusting to hear from you in the near future we beg to remain,
          Very truly yours,
          Pence Automobile Co.,

          *Maurice Wolfe*
          Mgr.

INGENIOUS YOUNG STUBBLE

A lonely-young fellow name Stubble
Made an "Auto" without any trouble.
  He went 'round selling soap,
  And he murmured, "I hoap
I can patent my little soap 'bubble.'"

Early in the century, even before the automobile had been completely accepted as the horse's successor, automobile racing caught the fancy of the people. The famous White racing steamer known as "Whistling Billy" (below, top), with Webb Jay at the wheel, lowered the world's record for the mile to 48⅗ seconds at Morris Park, New York, on July 4, 1905. When one considers that this record, considerably faster than a mile a minute, was established only five or six years after the average American had glimpsed his first automobile, it looms as an accomplishment of real proportions.

Also in 1905, George Herring (bottom) drove his neat little Stanley Steamer to victory on the Overland Race Track in Denver, Colorado, against several gasoline cars. Apparently Mr. Herring used the jockey crouch as a result of his studies of wind resistance.

## A Modern Gearshift in 1905

The engine on this 1905 Pierce Stanhope was mounted on a subframe just ahead of the rear axle. As in several early cars, the gearshift was on the steering column. The front seat—*not* the driver's seat—folded up when not in use. The car was advertised as "built primarily to stand the strenuous demands of a physician's work."

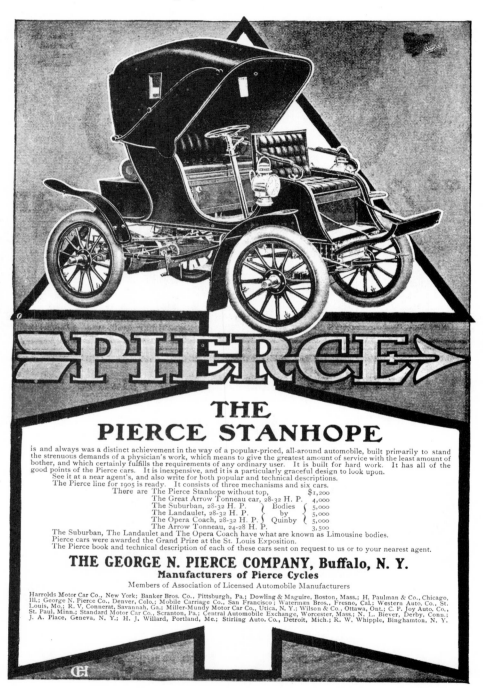

## THE PIERCE STANHOPE

is and always was a distinct achievement in the way of a popular-priced, all-around automobile, built primarily to stand the strenuous demands of a physician's work, which means to give the greatest amount of service with the least amount of bother, and which certainly fulfills the requirements of any ordinary user. It is built for hard work. It has all of the good points of the Pierce cars. It is inexpensive, and it is a particularly graceful design to look upon.

See it at a near agent's, and also write for both popular and technical descriptions.

The Pierce line for 1905 is ready. It consists of three mechanisms and six cars.

|  | | |
|---|---|---|
| There are The Pierce Stanhope without top, | | $1,200 |
| The Great Arrow Tonneau car, 28-32 H. P. | | 4,000 |
| The Suburban, 28-32 H. P. | Bodies | 5,000 |
| The Landaulet, 28-32 H. P. | by | 5,000 |
| The Opera Coach, 28-32 H. P. | Quinby | 5,000 |
| The Arrow Tonneau, 24-28 H. P. | | 3,500 |

The Suburban, The Landaulet and The Opera Coach have what are known as Limousine bodies.

Pierce cars were awarded the Grand Prize at the St. Louis Exposition.

The Pierce book and technical description of each of these cars sent on request to us or to your nearest agent.

### THE GEORGE N. PIERCE COMPANY, Buffalo, N. Y.
#### Manufacturers of Pierce Cycles
Members of Association of Licensed Automobile Manufacturers

Harrolds Motor Car Co., New York; Banker Bros. Co., Pittsburgh, Pa.; Dowling & Maguire, Boston, Mass.; H. Paulman & Co., Chicago, Ill.; George N. Pierce Co., Denver, Colo.; Mobile Carriage Co., San Francisco; Waterman Bros., Fresno, Cal.; Western Auto. Co., St. Louis, Mo.; R. V. Connerat, Savannah, Ga.; Miller-Mundy Motor Car Co., Utica, N. Y.; Wilson & Co., Ottawa, Ont.; C. P. Joy Auto. Co., St. Paul, Minn.; Standard Motor Car Co., Scranton, Pa.; Central Automobile Exchange, Worcester, Mass.; N. L. Biever, Derby, Conn.; J. A. Place, Geneva, N. Y.; H. J. Willard, Portland, Me.; Stirling Auto. Co., Detroit, Mich.; R. W. Whipple, Binghamton, N. Y.

By 1906 companies like Oldsmobile and Franklin (both pictured here) were manufacturing dependable, sturdy vehicles, yet the prejudice against automobiles continued. A Kansas City ordinance of 1904 required four qualifications of the motorist —"skill, experience, capacity, and sobriety"—and he had to prove it! Owners of automobiles were still plagued with laws that retarded the sale and operation of cars. An organization in Pennsylvania, the Farmers' Anti-Automobile Society, advised their members to patrol the highways on Sundays, shoot at motor-car drivers, and threaten them with arrest. In Fort Worth, Texas, any person riding or driving a horse or other domestic animal could, merely by putting up his hands, cause the machine to stop until the animals had passed. Each car had to have a bell or horn that could be heard 300 feet away.

The 1906 Model L Oldsmobile (top, right) had a 2-cycle engine with no valves, springs, camshafts, or gears. The Franklin (bottom, right) featured an air-cooled motor.

**The Franklin Light Tonneau**

Weight, 1250 pounds; 12 horse-power, four-cylinder, air-cooled motor, $1650.

# FRANKLIN

**The car you want** is not the car with the most horse-power, or with this frill or that, but the car that *does the most at the least expense*.

**The car you don't want** is the complicated, heavy car that wears out tires fast, uses gasoline extravagantly, costs a lot for repairs, and is clumsy besides.

**The Franklin 12 horse-power Light Tonneau** goes faster and better and smoother—on all roads—than most cars of 18 and 20 horse-power. It costs less to buy and less to maintain.

Water-cooled cars get their power by means of heavy motors and complicated parts. The Franklin gets its power by masterly engineering and its light,

**Four-cylinder, Air-cooled Motor**

It costs $1650, not $2000; but, even at $2,000, it would be cheaper than the others.

What does your horse-power cost? What does it do?

While you're thinking this over, look up the Franklin and some Franklin owners.

The picture below is the *Franklin 20 H. P. Touring-car.*

Send for book telling plain facts about the six 1905 *Franklins.*

Send for "Coast to Coast" Booklet, story of the Franklin's record from San Francisco to New York.

**H. H. Franklin Mfg. Co. Syracuse, N. Y.**

*Member Association Licensed Automobile Manufacturers*

## Car Equipment . . .

In 1906 one of the first American automobile shows was held at the Coliseum in Chicago. The sketches on these two pages appeared originally in a 1906 edition of the *Motor Way* magazine under the title "An Extraordinary Show." They show the various types of gear-shift levers, dashboard equipment, foot levers, and steering wheels exhibited. Practically all the drawings are of cars having both hand-operated throttles and spark-control levers. Some

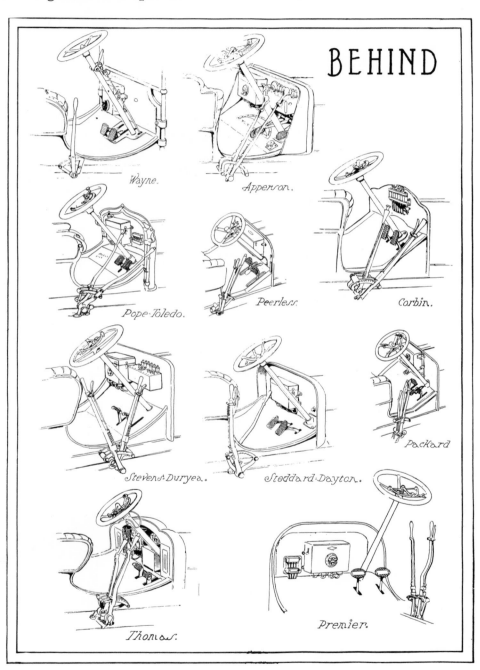

BEHIND

Wayne.

Apperson.

Pope-Toledo.

Peerless.

Corbin.

Stevens-Duryea.

Stoddard-Dayton.

Packard

Thomas.

Premier.

of the gearshift levers indicate selective-type transmissions, others are progressive-type, and still others are levers showing the operation of planetary-type transmissions. Some of the cars have coil boxes on the dashboard and many have sight-feed drip oilers. It is interesting to note that none of these prominent cars exhibited in 1906 had front doors. Of the twenty cars here sketched, Autocar, Reo, Packard, Ford, and Oldsmobile have stood the test of time.

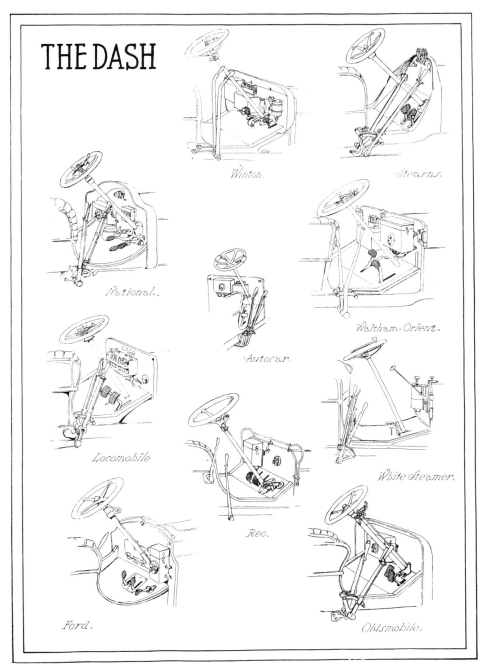

THE DASH

Winton.

Stearns.

National.

Waltham-Orient.

Autocar.

Locomobile

White Steamer.

Reo.

Ford.

Oldsmobile.

## The Chicago Coliseum, 1906

Automobile shows were an important factor in popularizing the automobile. The very first show was held in 1900 in Madison Square Garden, and 34 cars of all kinds—gas, steam, and electric—were exhibited. Auto shows became annual events at the Garden and at the Chicago Coliseum (below). The car is a 1906 Stevens-Duryea, part of the Coliseum exhibit.

An artist in 1906 has fun with the famous automobile personalities who attended the Chicago show. Notice Henry Ford, Number 16, without any pants, a barefoot Ransom E. Olds, Number 17, and Harvey Firestone, Number 13, with a tire about his waist. Charles E. Duryea, Number 7, who built his first car in 1893, was an old man compared to Ford.

1. JESSE FRENCH JR.
2. ROGER B. MCMULLEN
3. D. W. TWYMAN
4. A. L. RIKER
5. LOUIS WAINWRIGHT
6. PAT HUSSEY
7. CHAS. E. DURYEA
8. ELMER APPERSON
9. FRED L. SMITH
10. E. R. THOMAS
11. ALEXANDER WINTON
12. GEO. W. BENNETT
13. H. S. FIRESTONE
14. CHAS. B. SHANKS.
15. JIM COUZENS
16. HENRY FORD
17. R. E. OLDS

# The Baby Reo

When Ransom E. Olds took his initials R. E. O. and founded the Reo Company, he built a miniature car (below) in 1906 to exhibit around the country in various automobile shows. The car was an exact replica of the two-cylinder Reo of 1906 and operated on compressed air. The miniature car was picked up by Barnum and Bailey and exhibited and photographed with circus giants, wild-animal tamers, elephants, and midgets. It was a clever and colorful advertising stunt on the part of Mr. Olds and the Reo Company. The photograph on the top left shows the midget car behind the 1906 Reo after which it was modeled, standing in front of the Reo factory in Lansing.

These four cars, which were advertised so eloquently in 1905, have all disappeared. The Northern (bottom, left), so the story goes, was "silent and dustless."

**The Compound $1400**

**LIGHT TOURING CAR**

MODEL FOUR, 12-15 H.P.

This car is designed for people that want the best finish and workmanship that money can produce. Don't judge it by its price, but by comparison with other cars.

Our agency for your city may yet be unplaced. Let us hear from you.

**The E. H. V. Co. - Middletown, Conn.**

# THE MOLINE

**12 H.P.  Model D  $1,000**

Double opposed motor, 4½ in. bore and stroke, developing more than the rated horsepower. Detachable tonneau. Long wheel base. Easy riding springs. Best carburetor and ignition equipment. Thoroughly well proportioned, reliable and durable.

**Model "B"**—The lowest priced four-cylinder car that has "made good" this season. Stands long, hard runs and pleases our customers. **Price, $1,600.** Write for catalogue.

**MOLINE AUTOMOBILE CO., EAST MOLINE, ILL.**

Members American Motor Car Manufacturers' Association of Chicago.

**Northern**

**"SILENT AND DUSTLESS"**

*Quietest and easiest running car in the world*

**THE ONLY CAR WITH**

motor and entire mechanism, including crank shaft and transmission gear encased; with only one universal joint; with machinery tipped 12 degrees downward, throwing crank shaft on direct line to rear axle; with only three vital points to oil; with self-locking foot throttle; with 4-inch tires—at $1700.

**NO** Strut rods, truss rods, bolts, chains or gaskets. No oil tubes. No side levers, or any other attachments on body. No noise. No vibration. No dust.

All parts easily accessible. Never any need to crawl under car. Write for complete catalogue.

18 H. P., Side Entrance, $1700
Limousine Pattern . . $2500
Runabout, 7 H. P. . . $650

**NORTHERN MFG. CO., DETROIT, U. S. A.**
Member A. L. A. M.
NEW YORK CITY AGENT, PETER FOGARTY, 148 WEST 38th STREET

# The Gale Model A . . . $500

**IMMEDIATE DELIVERY**

Equipped with 28x3 Standard Single Tube Tires, Tool and Repair Kits—a Powerful, Practical, **Easy Riding** Runabout at a **Reasonable Price.**

**Model B $650**

Choice of any Standard Clincher Tires. Full Leather Buggy Top, Brass Side Lamps, Horn, Full Tool and Repair Kits, and with irreversible steering gear.

Both models have 5x6 water cooled motor, strong steel gear transmission, and four full elliptic 34-inch springs. Chain drive at side, close to bearings. Hinged body, which, by removal of two nuts and cotter pin, can be tilted to 50° angle. Everything on frame, which can be run without body, if desired.
☞ *Good Eastern and Southern territory still open.*

**The WESTERN TOOL WORKS**
**GALESBURG, ILLINOIS**

## A $250 Car, 1906

The Success, built and advertised (below) in 1906, was probably one of the cheapest cars in our history. It had a 2-horsepower gasoline motor and a speed of 4 to 18 miles per hour and would run 100 miles on a gallon of gasoline. It was designed on exactly the same lines as a buggy, with high buggy wheels and, for your $250, steel tires. Rubber tires were $25 extra.

An old American adage has it that the woman controls the purse strings. As early as 1906, auto manufacturers began to devise new ways and means of accommodating the female of the species. Obviously it was not appropriate for a long-skirted, full-busted, delicately coifed demoiselle to stand ankle-deep in mud, cranking away at her car. So in Plainfield, New Jersey, two brothers named Ball (below) invented a dashboard device to eliminate that backbreaking and most undignified chore of cranking.

Signs of a new business and a young industry: at the bottom of this 1906 advertisement for the Kansas City Motor Car, the company announces "opportunities for Live Agents."

## 57 Miles on a Gallon, 1907

Early car advertisements were full of such items as races, speed records, special awards, endurance and reliability marathons, coast-to-coast tours, hill climbs, and miles-per-gallon contests. A 1907 Reo (below) set a record by carrying four people 57 miles on one gallon of gas and the same four passengers 682 miles for $3.38 per person.

**REO** ..4-Seat.. Runabout **$675**

**Four people; 57 miles; 1¾ gallons of gasoline.**

That was the record (from Chicago to Cedar Lake, Ind., October 18th—the rain coming down in sheets). And the REO Runabout was the car that made it. 682 miles, 4 passengers; $3.38 per passenger. The REO Runabout also made this record and won the first prize gold medal in the famous six day New York Economy Test.

No other car could have made either of these records.

**REO** 5-Passenger Touring Car **$1250**

2-Passenger Runabout, $650
4-Passenger Runabout, $675

Write for the 1907 catalogue which describes it in detail. Also the REO $1250 five-passenger Touring Car.

**R. M. OWEN & CO., Lansing, Mich.**
(Sales Agents)

# 1907 GREAT SMITH CAR

**Price, $2500 F. O. B. Topeka**

Four cylinders, 4½ x 5 inches, water cooled engine, sliding gear transmission, three speeds forward and one reverse. 107 inch wheel base, 34 x 4 inch tires. Multiple disc clutch, ample tonneau, magnificent upholstery. Full elliptic unbreakable springs. Refrigerator in box at side. Ample room for extra tire, three powerful durable brakes

**In all respects a perfect machine— Built as well as any car in the world.**

**Smith Auto. Co., Topeka, Kansas, USA**
Makers of the World's Greatest $2500 Car.

**$1850** **Compare Kisselkar With Any Car That Costs Twice As Much**

DID you ever analyze Automobile Construction with reference to the cost? Has it ever occurred to you that it ought to be possible to put out a car—even a high-grade car—at considerably less than the prevailing prices? Well, that's just what Kisselkar was built to prove. And it has *proved* it. Let us show *you.*

**30 Horse Power Four Cylinders**

Kisselkar makes good in performance. That has been thoroughly demonstrated. The motor *must* develop at least 30 horse power under test before it is passed, and it often develops 32. It is noiseless, reliable, fast and powerful. It has shown its immense reserve time and again in the severest hill-climbing tests.

Makers: The Kissel Motor Car Co., Hartford, Wis.
Address all correspondence to
**McDUFFEE AUTOMOBILE COMPANY, Sole Agents**
CHICAGO, Michigan Ave. at 15th St.    MILWAUKEE, 228-230-232 Wisconsin St.

Although modern motorists have come to accept water cooling as standard equipment, once upon a time air cooling was just as popular with car manufacturers. The Knox, the Victor, the Aerocar, the Franklin, and the Adams-Farwell (below) all used air-cooling systems. An air-cooling system required no radiator, no water pump, no hoses, and no connections. There was no need to worry about freezing radiators. The Franklin firm made many long-distance tests and endurance runs with their cars sealed in low or second gear to prove the dependability of air cooling. In Europe there are still a number of small air-cooled automobiles being manufactured.

The air-cooled Adams-Farwell (below), built in Dubuque, Iowa, in 1907, had a revolving engine of five cylinders and a four-speed selective transmission with two clutches. According to advertisements, it required no skill to operate and it was impossible to engage both clutches at the same time. The two photos (bottom, left) show the chassis of this revolving-cylinder motor car and (bottom) its transmission gear and controlling mechanism.

The Lambert in 1907 (bottom, right) came up with a friction drive transmission and also one of history's worst slogans—"It's a stronger proposition than you have imagined."

## The Gale and Mr. Willys, 1907

The 1907 Gale "climbed hills like a squirrel and ate up the road like an express train" (40 miles per hour fully loaded). It had "beautiful lines, a tilted body" (which they accused other manufacturers of copying) and "more power than any other car on the market." It also had as many struts and braces (see cut) as an early biplane.

The man who put his name to the 1907 Detroit ad (bottom) is the same John N. Willys who later built the Willys car, the Willys Overland, and whose company built the famous Army Jeep which played such a big part in World War II. After Mr. Willys had successfully demonstrated his ability as a supersalesman for the Detroit Auto Vehicle Company, he rescued the Overland Company of Indianapolis from bankruptcy with $500 to meet a payroll, and eventually it became the Willys Overland Company of Toledo.

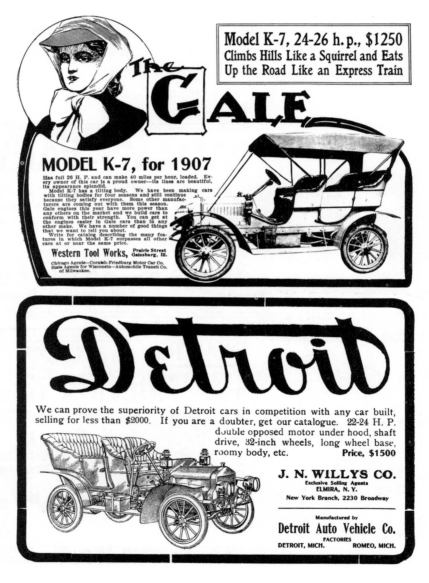

The 1907 letter from Henry Ford to the Holley Magneto firm is interesting for the lack of stenographer's initials—which leads one to believe that Henry typed and signed the letter himself—and also for the names of the Ford organization officers in the upper left-hand corner of the stationery. Vice-president John F. Dodge was one of the later well-known Dodge brothers, and secretary and treasurer James Couzens eventually became United States Senator from Michigan. Ford's early economizing is also interesting, as manifested by his blocking out the names of the former company officials and putting in the new officers underneath, instead of investing in new stationery.

The Model car, built in Peru, Indiana, in 1907 was an all-purpose car with a detachable body. It could be used as either a five-passenger family car or a two-passenger runabout.

The above letter is self-explanatory. The Ford Car which won the 24-hour race in Detroit, Saturday, June 22d, was equipped with a Holley Magneto. During the entire race the magneto was in constant use. The battery was never used, and the magneto was not repaired or adjusted in any manner whatever. A severe test like this in public proves conclusively that the Holley Magneto is not equalled by any ignition device in the world. Several of the contesting cars were equipped with foreign-made magnetos.

**Holley Brothers Co.**

# FAMOUS FIRST CARS

ALTHOUGH inventors had tinkered with the idea of the horseless carriage for a century and George B. Selden had plans to propel a vehicle by a gasoline engine in 1877, it was not until 1900 that practical mechanics such as Henry Ford, Ransom E. Olds, and James Ward Packard began to visualize these contraptions as marketable items and money-making propositions. These were the men who lent their names to their inventions—Ford, Olds, Buick, Studebaker, the Dodge Brothers, Packard—and who today, 50 years later, would probably have difficulty recognizing the vehicles which now bear their names.

It is difficult to believe that the sleek, powerful Ford of today is a blood relative of the two-cylinder, five-hundred-pound relic (below, top) which Mr. Ford built in 1895–1896. This first Ford had a three-gallon gas tank under the seat, could attain a speed of 20 miles per hour, and had no reverse. The car was built in a shed at 58 Bagley Avenue in Detroit, exactly where the Michigan Theatre now stands.

One day in August, 1898, a dissatisfied car owner named James Ward Packard confronted Alexander Winton, bicycle and automobile manufacturer, over his desk in Cleveland, Ohio.

Packard had purchased the twelfth automobile made by Winton, and as he drove it to his home in Warren, Ohio, the machine had broken down many times and he had to be hauled in by a team of horses. Packard had a number of suggestions for Winton, but the latter, impatient and annoyed, snapped back, "Mr. Packard, if you are so smart, why don't you make a car yourself?"

Of course Packard did. His first car (right, bottom) was completed November 6, 1899. A single-seater, buggy type with wire wheels, it steered by means of a tiller and had a single-cylinder horizontal engine which developed 12 horsepower. The transmission had three speeds forward and one reverse, which was considered a great innovation at that time.

58

The three oldest automotive concerns still in existence in the United States are Oldsmobile, Packard, and Studebaker. The first Studebaker offered for sale to the public was an electric runabout built in 1902 (below, top). It was powered by a 24-cell battery and had four forward speeds of 3, 5, 9, and 13 miles per hour. It was only 73 inches long and 29 inches wide.

The 6-Cylinder, Reasonably Priced **de Soto Six** 55 H.P.

The car with a **stronger appeal** than any recent product of the trade—the one that meets a popular demand. We have an unusually attractive proposition for dealers. Write at once for free catalog and full particulars.

Sells for $2,185

de Soto Motor Car Company, Auburn, Ind.

David Dunbar Buick was an inventor who amassed at least fifty fortunes for other and often lesser men but died a poor man. The first Buick, a two-cylinder 21-horsepower car, was built in 1903, and in 1904 he produced and sold 37 automobiles. The 1904 Buick is pictured at left, middle. Buick, an inventor of great versatility, contributed to modernity a lawn sprinkler, an enameled bathtub, and a number of gadgets that had to do with indoor toilets. In 1905 William C. Durant, the financial wizard of Flint, Michigan, succeeded in interesting the solid citizens of that town in the marketing possibilities of Buick's automobile and was able to amass such capital that by 1910 Buick was one of the top 10 car makers in the United States. Durant hired such famous auto names as Charles W. Nash, Walter P. Chrysler, and Louis Chevrolet to help in the Buick operation, and in 1908 he organized General Motors. Somehow the man with the original idea, David D. Buick, passed out of the picture.

The present De Soto is of relatively recent vintage. The first De Soto (left, bottom) was built in 1913 at Auburn, Indiana, but not by Mr. Chrysler, as many people might assume.

59

## The Studebakers and the Dodge Brothers

The history of the Studebaker family is one of the most interesting connected with the automotive trade. In 1853 one John Mohler Studebaker of South Bend, Indiana, joined in the California gold rush and, like so many others, lost both his shirt and his love for speculation. He opened a blacksmith's shop. On the side he started making wheelbarrows. The wheelbarrows developed into the Studebaker wagon business, and John Studebaker and his brothers eventually became the largest wagon producers in the country, supplying vehicles to the Mormons for their trek to Salt Lake City and all sorts of carts to the Union forces during the Civil War. Soon there was a world-wide market for every type of Studebaker horse-drawn vehicle.

Since the family had devoted so much of its time and energy over the years to different modes of transportation, it was natural that the Studebakers should jump into the automobile business as soon as it came along. After all, a car was simply a cart without a horse. In 1899 they started making bodies for electric passenger cars, and in 1902 they had patented their own electric car and truck. The first gasoline Studebaker (below, top) was a 1904 touring car which seated five persons and sold for $1,750. It had a two-cylinder 17-horsepower engine with two speeds forward, one reverse.

The Dodge brothers, John and Horace, started their long and successful career in the automobile industry as manufacturers of motors and transmissions for Henry Ford. Many believe today that it was the excellent mechanical work the Dodge brothers did on the Ford early in the industry's life that did much to establish the name of Ford in public favor. It was not until 1914 that they attached their own name to a product of their mechanical wizardry. The 1914 Dodge (left, bottom) was the first car in the industry with an all-steel body and the forerunner of the first all-steel closed car, also manufactured by Dodge. They produced 249 cars in 1914, 45,033 in 1915.

60

THEY were still making fun of the automobile in 1906, as Paderewsky's pianomobile (below, left) and the horse-automobile compromise (below, right) bear witness (*Life* cartoons, 1906). One of the important departments in which cars had to excel was hill climbing. An early Cadillac ad boasted that "no grade was prohibitive," and a popular method of demonstrating this pulling power was to drive the car up a steep ramp. A 1906 Leader car makes the ascent (middle, left) at an Indiana State Fair. The Black Motor Company in 1908 did a little jazzed-up advertising (middle, right) for its Motor Runabout which had "Speed! I Guess Yes!" At bottom is an illustration of the friction drive used in the Cartercar.

Bjones, who is fond of his horses, and has had much trouble with his automobiles, decides to compromise the matter.

61

Murine, "a tonic for the 'Auto Eye,'" came up in 1907 with one of the most intriguing ads in the history of huckstering, entitled "Charles the Chauffeur."

# Charles the Chauffeur

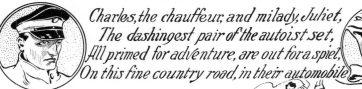

Charles, the chauffeur, and milady, Juliet,
The dashingest pair of the autoist set,
All primed for adventure, are out for a spiel,
On this fine country road, in their automobile.

As they dash down the pike, without quaver or hitch,
The farmers in front of them take to the ditch
And the cohorts that follow are trailing afar
Like the Netherby clan after young Lochinvar.

After climbing a long grassy slope, at the top
The pulsing machine has been brought to a stop,
For the silt of the air, and microbic flies
Have reddened the lids of milady's bright eyes.

And Charles, at the signal, has stopped the machine
And passed back the bottle containing Murine
So milady leans back, and looks up at the sky
As the magic "two-drops" are dropped into each eye.

Now again they are off, at a forty mile pace,
With vision restored and new zest in the race;
And woe betide him who opposes their gait,
For he's booked for a serious tussle with fate.

The automobile, by some unwritten code,
Has won, in fee simple, all rights to the road;
And quite as true title indisputably, lies,
To the trite, but true saying, "Murine cures eyes"

**MURINE** IS A TONIC FOR THE "AUTO EYE,"
SOOTHES AND QUICKLY CURES EYES
INFLAMED BY EXPOSURE TO STRONG WINDS AND DUST

By 1907 the price range of automobiles was not yet within the reach of the upper middle class but it was getting there. Two of the cars below sold for $600.

## Stanhope $800
## Runabout $600

JEWEL argument is not a matter of superlatives nor extravagant, boastful claims. It is based upon these definite points:

There is no other gasoline car that is so easily controlled.

There is no other gasoline motor so simple.

There is no other gasoline car that costs so little for repairs and maintenance expense.

Let us give you the whole story of JEWEL construction and equipment in our free booklet. It fully describes the JEWEL Valveless, Two-cycle engine, and shows why experience, rather than advertising, has made the JEWEL famous.

**FOREST CITY MOTOR CAR CO.**

**136 Walnut St., Massillon, Ohio, U. S. A.**

An Ideal Car for
**Business and Professional Men**

## The FEDERAL

**Model C-Runabout, $600**

A car for every day service, constructed upon the simplest lines to attain the maximum of power, speed and durability, and needs no mechanical knowledge to operate it successfully.

*It is a car of style and practicability*

If you are contemplating the purchase of a car, *this is the car for you to buy.*

*Dealers, this is the car for you to handle.*
Write for full particulars.

**Federal Automobile Co.**
40th St. and Wentworth Ave., Chicago, Ill.

## The MARVEL
## Automobile Roadster

**The Greatest Value on the Market
A Car of Superior Merit
Gives Most Satisfactory Service**
WRITE FOR FULL PARTICULARS

## Marvel Motor Car Co.
**284-290 Rivard St., DETROIT, MICH.**

## Colt

## $1,500
## Six-cylinder Runabout
### 40 H.P., 60 miles an hour

Bore, 4 1-2"     Stroke, 5"     Weight, 1,800 lbs.

The Colt six-cylinder runabout is the sensation of the year. It is so beautiful in design, so attractive in finish, that one is apt to slip over its wonderful mechanical qualities. Its extreme speed, better than a mile-a-minute, fits it for every purpose for which the $4,000 and $5,000 semi-racing cars are made. Its 40 h.p six-cylinder engine provides a tremendous power in a steady, even torque that enables it to run away on the hills from any runabout of the season, bar none.

### COLT RUNABOUT CO.

**Offices, Motor Mart, 1876 Broadway at 62d St.
Factory, Yonkers.**

══ **New York** ══

63

## Oakland and Olds, 1907

The Oakland Car, which later became the Pontiac (now one of General Motors' cars), is remembered by car fans for once having a V-8 engine (in 1916). In 1923 the Oakland Company became the first to use Duco instead of paint or varnish, and the 1907 Oakland (below, top) had a new variety of engine that rotated in a counterclockwise direction.

In 1907, a year of business panic and closing banks, the Oldsmobile Company came out with the Palace Touring Car (below, bottom), one of the first automobiles to have any kind of enclosure for driver and front-seat passenger.

64

The idea of the all-purpose automobile was developed by Charles E. Duryea in 1907. The two cars advertised below are really the same car, the Duryea Phaeton. On the left it is a runabout with a shelf in the rear for tying on baggage; and on the right it is a touring car with the rear seat open instead of closed and the leather top stretched back to cover both seats.

The very first cars that Charles Duryea made after his earlier association with brother Frank had two rear wheels and only one in front. The body looked something like a horn of plenty, each side formed to resemble a mermaid. This rather grotesque-looking little car had a control stick at the driver's left hand that was similar to the control stick on some of our early airplanes. The car did something with every movement of the stick—usually something unexpected. Charles Duryea once drove this odd-looking car to the top of Mount Penn, an ascent full of steep grades and hairpin turns, in high gear. Despite this fine performance, he soon compromised with orthodoxy and added another wheel in front. Four-wheel cars are the only type that have stood the test of time.

# DURYEA— the car with 15 years of experience in it.

## THE DURYEA,

the car with fifteen years' experience. We have largely increased our output for 1907, and will be in excellent position to take care of the wants of our agents. DURYEA CARS have always been reliable, and the improvements for 1907 will make them even more satisfactory than they have been in the past. This is saying a great deal, because any Duryea agent or owner will tell you that for reliability and general utility the DURYEA Car is unexcelled.

**DURYEA PHAETON** (Rear Seat Open.)

This is the same automobile illustrated on the opposite page but with the rear seat open instead of closed and with double top, the rear part of the top detachable. We are also manufacturing for the coming season a Double Victoria, price $2500. This car will be very popular for touring as it is large, roomy and powerful. Illustrations will be ready at an early date. If interested, write for photographs and other details.

The DURYEA CARS are the result of a great many years of experience, and embody the ideas of a man who is considered an expert authority on automobile construction. The two important features to be considered when buying an automobile are the first price and the cost of up-keep. Considering carrying capacity, touring, general utility and cost, the DURYEA CAR is as low in price as is consistent with good material and workmanship. The low cost of maintenance is a strong talking point of the DURYEA CAR. We have numerous letters from our agents which prove that both in consumption of gasoline and oil, the DURYEA CARS give the maximum mileage at minimum expense. Write for detailed information.

**Price, $1,550. DURYEA PHAETON.** (Rear Seat Closed.)

This is the best automobile for the man who wants both a runabout and a touring car. It is interchangeable by lifting the rear seat.

# DURYEA POWER CO., READING, PA., U. S. A.

*The Haynes, 1893 and 1907*

Here is the Haynes Automobile Company's 1907 version of the invention of the automobile
—by Elwood Haynes, of course. The 1893 and 1907 models make an interesting comparison.

# THE STORY OF THE HAYNES

THIRTEEN years have passed since Elwood Haynes began to work on the theory that a "Horseless carriage" could be propelled satisfactorily by a gas engine.

The result in 1893 was the first American gasoline automobile.

**Elwood Haynes**

As pictured here, it shows small resemblance to the well-known cars that bear the Haynes name for 1907, but it contains elements of design that are now standard, and to this antiquated vehicle every modern automobile is, in some respect, in debt. With this car, Elwood Haynes proved his theory—the car would run—and it will run today. Its active life was closed only recently when the Smithsonian Institute secured it for its Museum to illustrate the history of the automobile.

Since 1893 there have been many Haynes cars—a steady progression leading down to the Model S and T of 1907. It has taken time to develop the automobile, and Haynes had a long start.

The original leadership has never been lost.

The Haynes factory was the first automobile factory to be built in America. Low tension make-and-break ignition originated in the Haynes models of 1895. The Haynes began the march of improvements in materials by introducing nickel steel. Aluminum alloy for bodies and for engine parts was used first in the Haynes. The Haynes were the first cars to be equipped with large wheels. The

**Model T. 50 H. P., 4 Cylinders, Seats 7, Direct Drive, $3,500**

models are still ahead of their rivals, embodying devices that will be imitated in other cars in later years.

The Vanderbilt Elimination Race proved the quality of a Haynes when a regular stock model—the only stock model entered—won its

place on the American Team against the best special designs America could produce.

In the final Cup Race, against special racing cars of twice its horse-power, its wonderful showing is too well known to need repeating.

**Model S. 30 H. P., 4 Cylinders. Direct Drive, Seats 5, $2,500**

side entrance body was a Haynes introduction. In a multitude of details the Haynes has been universally imitated. There is no doubt but that the Haynes has been more copied *from* than any other car.

To-day in their simplicity, reliability and perfection the Haynes

**The Haynes of 1893**

In all types, roller bearings all along the power route from piston stroke to hub.

When you drive a Haynes you drive America's best—and that *now means* the best in the world.

## HAYNES AUTOMOBILE COMPANY, Kokomo, Indiana
### Oldest Automobile Manufacturers in America.    Members A. L. A. M.

NEW YORK
1715 Broadway

**HAYNES**

CHICAGO
1420
Michigan Ave.

The first Plymouth automobile was manufactured as early as 1908, but not by Chrysler. The Commercial Motor Truck Company (right) of Plymouth, Ohio, were producers of a friction-driven Plymouth car.

In 1907 there were 2,500 four-cylinder Ford Runabouts (bottom, right) on the road. A year later Ford put out his now immortal "Tin Lizzie," the Model T.

During the pioneer period there were many conflicting opinions regarding the best design. As the gasoline engine began to attain uncontested supremacy over steam and electricity, other controversies sprang up in its stead: chain- *versus* shaft-driven cars; four-cylinder *versus* six-cylinder engines; high wheels with solid tires *versus* low wheels with pneumatic tires; and water-cooling systems *versus* air cooling. One of the advocates of the latter was the Knox Waterless (below, left) of Springfield.

In 1908 a Cincinnati lawyer by the name of William Howard Taft—a huge man with a walrus mustache who reportedly ate steak for breakfast—was elected President of the United States. That same year the Maxwell Company, which was later to become a part of the great Chrysler Corporation, advertised a 14-horsepower Runabout (below, left) and recommended it to the "doctor, lawyer, contractor, city and suburban salesman, builder, businessman; in fact to everyone whose needs do not exceed economical, safe, and speedy transportation for two."

Although electric lights were used by many Americans during the term of office of this rotund President who ate big breakfasts, the motorists of his time still relied upon kerosene and gas lamps. The most famous concern specializing in this type of auto accessory was the Solar Company (below, right). When gas generators were used, the water dripped from above onto carbide, resulting in a gas that was carried to the head lamps through copper and rubber tubing. Later the famous Prest-O-Lite tanks became extremely popular. These tanks carried enough gas for several hours' use.

As odd as the car with three wheels, or the chassis that looks like a horn of plenty, or the car that travels on compressed air, or the self-propelled baby carriage that runs by springs—as odd as these seems this 1908 advertisement for a tire cover with "oval-headed steel rivets set closely along the sides." The steel rivets were supposed to save wear and tear on the tires, especially "on rocky and rutty roads." They were "puncture-proof against nails, sharp stones, or glass" and made "skidding practically impossible."

# WOODWORTH TREAD
## FOR 1908
### A SURE PROTECTION FOR AUTOMOBILE TIRES

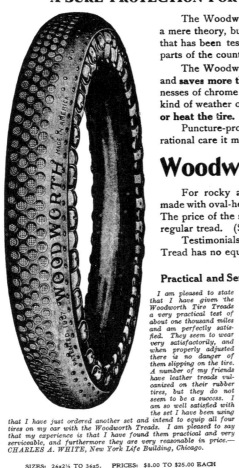

The Woodworth Tread is not a new untried novelty or a mere theory, but a sensible, practical, useful tire protector that has been tested for years on thousands of cars in all parts of the country and under all possible conditions.

The Woodworth Tread puts an end to all tire troubles and **saves more than half the tire bill.** Made of three thicknesses of chrome leather that will **not stretch or crack** in any kind of weather or hard usage, and **positively will not chafe or heat the tire.**

Puncture-proof against nails, sharp stones or glass. With rational care it makes skidding practically impossible.

## Woodworth Special Tread

For rocky and rutty roads a special tread has been made with oval-headed steel rivets, set closely along the sides. The price of the special tread is 20 per cent. more than the regular tread. (See illustration.)

Testimonials from thousands prove that the Woodworth Tread has no equal for safety, durability and economy.

### Practical and Serviceable; Reasonable in Price

*I am pleased to state that I have given the Woodworth Tire Treads a very practical test of about one thousand miles and am perfectly satisfied. They seem to wear very satisfactorily, and when properly adjusted there is no danger of them slipping on the tire. A number of my friends have leather treads vulcanized on their rubber tires, but they do not seem to be a success. I am so well satisfied with the set I have been using that I have just ordered another set and intend to equip all four tires on my car with the Woodworth Treads. I am pleased to say that my experience is that I have found them practical and very serviceable, and furthermore they are very reasonable in price.— CHARLES A. WHITE, New York Life Building, Chicago.*

SIZES: 26x2½ TO 36x5.    PRICES: $8.00 TO $25.00 EACH
WRITE FOR CATALOG

## LEATHER TIRE GOODS CO., Newton Upper Falls, Mass.

Denver Auto Goods Co., Distributors, 1614 Broadway, Denver, Col.    California Distributors, Chanslor & Lyon, San Francisco and Los Angeles.
Ballou & Wright, 86 Sixth Street, Portland, Ore., Distributors for the State of Oregon.

# The Glidden Tours

In the early years of the automobile industry, the horseless carriage had to win its difficult way into the life of Mr. Average American. A wealthy New England industrialist by the name of Charles J. Glidden, who had made a round-the-world tour of 50,000 miles in an English Napier, dedicated his life and fortune to popularizing automotive transportation in the United States. He had leisure and money and was an enthusiastic motorist. Long before he established his now famous Glidden Tours, he spent many hours chugging painfully and slowly through the mudholes that the State of New York chose to call roads. Perhaps he was lonely on those long stretches of open road between New York and Philadelphia. Perhaps he took delight in luring unsuspecting sportsmen out to those vast stretches of muddy highway. Perhaps he really believed in the joys of the open road.

In 1905 the automobile manufacturers joined the American Automobile Association in sponsoring cross-country Reliability Tours to sell the public on the practicality and inevitability of automobiles. Mr. Glidden offered a trophy for the winner of each event, and from that time on the Reliability Tours were known as the Glidden Tours and were held annually. From 1905 to 1913 they were highly competitive events in which almost every automobile manufacturer entered one or more cars.

The early tours were charted over mountains, through forests, across barren stretches, and under conditions of mud, dust, stormy weather, and rocky roads that would keep the modern motorist tucked safely in his warm, dry bed. Millions of people witnessed the contests as the weather-beaten drivers passed through every type of area—urban and rural.

### A A A RELIABILITY ROAD TESTS
#### GLIDDEN TROPHY TOURS

| Year | Itinerary | Mileage | Time | Winner |
|---|---|---|---|---|
| 1904 | New York to St. Louis | 966 | .... | Napier ° |
| 1905 | New York, Hartford, Bretton Woods, Worcester, New York | 870 | 7 days | Pierce-Arrow |
| 1906 | Buffalo, Saratoga, Montreal, Quebec, Bretton Woods | 1,035 | 12 days | Pierce-Arrow |
| 1907 | Cleveland, Chicago, Indianapolis, Columbiana, Pittsburgh, New York | 1,519 | 15 days | Buffalo Auto Club |
| 1908 | Buffalo, Pittsburgh, Philadelphia, Albany, Boston, Portland, Saratoga | 1,685 | 14 days | Pierce-Arrow |
| 1909 | Detroit, Chicago, Minneapolis, Denver, Salina, Kansas City | 2,639 | 15 days | Pierce-Arrow |
| 1910 | Cincinnati, Louisville, Fort Worth, Omaha, Chicago | 2,851 | 16 days | Premier |
| 1911 | New York, Atlanta, Jacksonville | 1,396 | 12 days | Maxwell |
| 1912 | Detroit, Indianapolis, Louisville, Memphis, Baton Rouge, New Orleans | 1,272 | 12 days | Maxwell |
| 1913 | Minneapolis to Glacier Park, Montana | 1,300 | 8 days | Locomobile |

° Driven by Charles J. Glidden.

Prominent people in the automobile industry saw possibilities in the Glidden Tours. If the American public could be attracted to the open road, the Fords and Firestones would of a certainty sell more cars and tires. In 1907 Harvey Firestone furnished the Glidden Tourists with roadside lunches at his farm home near Columbiana, Ohio.

In 1946 a reenactment of the Glidden Tour was held from New York City and Boston to Cleveland, Ohio, via Detroit. Below is a photograph taken at that same Firestone Homestead, where the 1946 Tourists, driving some 75 antique cars, participated in a noonday lunch as guest of Harvey S. Firestone, Jr. At the left is James Melton, opera singer, radio artist, and collector of antique automobiles; behind the wheel of a 1907 International high-wheeled Auto-Buggy is Mr. Firestone; and the gentleman on the right is Major Augustus Post, an official of the original Glidden Tour who drove a White Steamer in the early contests.

## Glidden Tourists Were Hardy

The central idea behind the tours was that they be held in different parts of the country each year under different conditions of terrain and weather. One year the tourists would chase each other over mountains, the next year through swamps. One year they would be soaked in torrential rains, the next they would run out of water on the Western plains. The idea was to convince the public of the exquisite pleasure of automobile travel. Despite the hardships that the early tourists underwent, there can be no doubt that Mr. Glidden's pet project proved a direct inspiration to the road builders who went on to construct our unsurpassed highway system.

The tour of 1905 meandered on twisting, winding roads from New York to Bretton Woods, New Hampshire. Bad roads, imperfect machines, and inclement weather were not the only hazards. The shrewd villagers along the way, who disliked automobiles anyway, fined the contestants for speeding or disturbing the peace, charged exorbitant fees to have damaged automobiles towed into town, and even, it was reported, contrived accidents when natural ones did not occur.

In the photograph at top left, a White Steamer splashes through a typical stretch of road during the 1908 tour. Below, a Packard entry the same year glides serenely along a country road. At bottom, Charles J. Glidden (right) and Major Augustus Post, famous balloonist.

THE Glidden Tour was not the only trick the auto industry had up its sleeve to advertise and popularize its product. Hill-climbing contests and races were equally important. In 1908 George Robertson drove his 90-horsepower Locomobile No. 16 for 258 miles to win the famous Vanderbilt Cup Race on Long Island. In spite of bad weather his speed of 64.3 miles per hour broke all existing records. The top photo below shows Robertson (at the wheel) and his mechanic Glenn Etheridge in 1908. In a 1948 photo (bottom) the same George Robertson is shown at the wheel. The car is now owned by artist Peter Helck.

## Versatile Studebaker

Studebaker in 1908 presented the Suburban, an "adaptable car." By merely rearranging seats, trunk, and top, it could be made into a "runabout," a "passenger and baggage car," or a "light four-passenger car, a vehicle to use every day in half a dozen ways."

Introducing the *Studebaker* "Suburban" THE ADAPTABLE CAR

AS A SMART RUNABOUT

COMBINATION PASSENGER AND BAGGAGE CAR

AS A LIGHT FOUR PASSENGER CAR

**W**HEN EQUIPPED with regular rear seat, a light four-passenger touring car; rear seat removed (can be done in a moment) and rumble seat substituted, a smart runabout; without rear or rumble seat, a combination passenger and baggage car.

## *A necessary adjunct to every suburban or country home*

The Studebaker "Suburban" is adaptable to numerous uses that will readily suggest themselves.

For instance: When your home is located at a distance from the railway station and you have a visitor arriving on a late train, you can remove the rear seat and, if you wish, bring home your visitor and his baggage in one trip; or, if there is a party you can send your man back to the station for their baggage.

Your baggage can be carried to the beach in your "Suburban."

It is just the car for a hunting, fishing or other outing trip, for running out to the golf or country club as a light four-passenger touring car or as a smart runabout.

The Studebaker "Suburban" is a car you will use every day in half a dozen different ways — it is literally the *adaptable* car.

The Studebaker "Suburban" chassis is identical with that of the regular Studebaker "30" touring car, which is a sufficient guarantee that from a mechanical standpoint the car will give satisfactory service.

*Write for full description of the Studebaker "Suburban" and other gasolene and electric models.*

## Studebaker Automobile Co., Main Factory South Bend, Ind. General Office Cleveland, O.

BRANCHES:

Boston, Mass.—Studebaker Bros. Co. of New York, 1020 Boylston Street (Sub Branch)
Chicago, Ill.—Studebaker Bros. Mfg. Co., 378-388 Wabash Avenue
Cleveland, Ohio—Studebaker Automobile Co., 2064 Euclid Avenue
Dallas, Texas—Studebaker Bros. Mfg. Co., 317-319 Elm Street
Denver, Colo.—Studebaker Automobile Co., 1536 Broadway
Kansas City, Mo.—Studebaker Bros. Mfg. Co., 13th and Hickory Streets

New York City—Studebaker Bros. Co. of New York, Broadway and 48th Street
Philadelphia, Pa.—Studebaker Bros. Co. of New York, 240 North Broad Street (Sub Branch)
Portland, Ore.—Studebaker Bros. Co. Northwest, 330-336 East Morrison Street
Salt Lake City, Utah—Studebaker Bros. Co. of Utah, 157 State Street
San Francisco, Cal.—Studebaker Bros. Co. of California, Mission and Fremont Streets
Seattle, Wash.—Studebaker Bros. Co. Northwest, 308 F st Avenue, So. (Sub Branch)

The year 1908 was a big one for cars. Buick produced a $1,750 four-cylinder Model D (top photo) and manufactured 543 of them. Henry Ford built his first Model T (below) with a steering wheel on the left and a two-speed planetary transmission.

## Hill-climb Contest

On April 8, 1908, Walter C. White (below, top), driving a White Steamer, won the Fort George Hill Climb in New York City in 32½ seconds. Seventy other cars were defeated by the White Steamer in a climb of 1,900 feet up an 11 per cent grade from a standing start. This was one of the most notable hill-climbing contests held in America, and for months the White Company advertised the great pulling power of its winning automobile.

An outstanding car in 1908 was the Model 34 Rambler (bottom photo), manufactured in Kenosha, Wisconsin. The engine developed 32.4 horsepower and the car weighed 2,800 lb. The Rambler later became the Jeffery and finally the Nash.

The 1908 A.B.C. (right, above) was a high-off-the-ground auto with carriage wheels and a single-chain drive. This car was equipped with (or blinded by) one of the first windshields. The shield was made of leather and isinglass, could be rolled up when not in use, and probably reduced the driver's visibility to almost zero.

The Glidden Tours not only bred a competitive spirit in rival auto manufacturers but gave them an area for combat. The 1908 Maxwell ad (below, right) angrily challenges the winner of the Glidden Tour of that year to a coast-to-coast "endurance run" from New York to San Francisco, with a purse of $5,000 at stake. It is a little obscure as to why the Maxwell people were so upset. It seems that the light and inexpensive Maxwells had won several Tours in the past, but now "the Glidden Tour rules had been so modified as to let the high-priced cars down easy if they lose." The Maxwell people decided to sulk and later challenged the Tour winner to this cross-country dual race. No one accepted the challenge, and apparently no broken heads resulted from the feud.

# The Well-Equipped Motorist

EARLY in the century an automobile trip was not the casual street-clothes affair it is today. All types of special costumes and protective devices were necessary if m'lady and her spouse wished to descend from their voyage looking neat and snappy. There were special visored caps and leather cloaks, rubberized suits and dresses, goggles and dust coats and auto robes and storm aprons. Magazines such as *The Automobile* and *Motor Age* wrote articles on "What the Well Dressed Autoist Now Wears" and "How to Stay Stylish in an Open Car." They went into great detail, even describing what the female motorist should wear "to race meets and hill climbs in a fashionable locality . . . it is necessary to wear a hat of as dainty a character as possible, commensurate with the sport. Many women, after long-and-costly experiments with motoring headgear, have fallen back on the dust and rain resisting Panama. A visored cap is very smart headgear but be sure it precisely matches the coat . . ." (*The Automobile*, September 3, 1908.)

The gentleman at top, left, seems well protected behind his mustache and under his Miller Tourist cap. The washer (below, right) is scrubbing up in a Collapsible Rubber Auto Wash Basin especially handy to remedy "the soiled condition of the hands after making adjustments or repairs on the road . . . convenient to carry folded up like an opera hat . . . and in cold weather it is filled with hot water and used as a foot warmer."

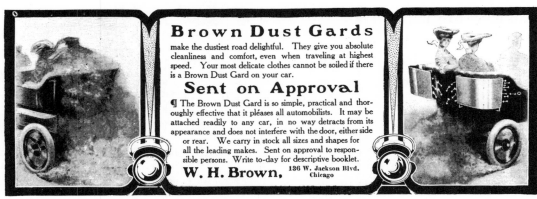

78

## MANY PEOPLE

Patented in U. S. Nov. 15, '04
Patented in Canada Nov. 8, '04

are troubled with bronchial and throat afflictions during the cold weather, and remain indoors the greater part of the winter.
¶ If a Scott Muffler is worn when going out, those susceptible to zero weather will find that the Scott Muffler

### MAKES ZERO WEATHER PLEASANT.

¶ They are neat and attractive, and really add to one's appearance.
¶ They can be taken off—not over the head—unfastened at the back—and put in the pocket, when not required for use.
¶ Our illustrated booklet tells all about them—prices, too. It will be sent as soon as you send for it.

## The Scott Muffler Co., 175 Main St., Portsmouth, Ohio.

Brown Dust Guards (page 78), which seem to attack the problem at the source, "make the dustiest road delightful." In the days of open cars, shrewd manufacturers of automobile accessories emphasized bronchial diseases, throat infections, head colds, and pneumonia. Thus the Scott Muffler Company (above) wanted to sell the motorist those frightening men-from-Mars goggles and mask to make "zero weather pleasant" and had the nerve to call their product "neat and attractive." The rubberized storm apron (left) had five holes in it for the heads of the five occupants of the car. The well-equipped driver always carried this waterproof robe under the seat or in his tool box for protection against the rains. Each hole had a collar, and all five collars could be buttoned securely around the necks of the occupants. The fashionable motorists on the right, with the fur robe and muff, are prepared for cold weather but not for rain.

# Milady's Fashions

THERE was heated controversy in 1914 as to where Milady's motor styles originated, Paris or New York. An ad in *The Automobile* of January 15, 1914, stated categorically that "even the most patriotic American will admit that motor styles originate in Paris. The small-town, Middle Western merchant looks to Chicago for his ideas in style. Chicago goes to

New York, New York depends on London, and London gets ideas from Paris."

The motorist's lady needed clothes that would withstand the dust when it was dry, the rain when it was wet, and the wind always. Open, roofless autos made early female car-fans more practical than they are today. Rubberized garments and dust repellers and hats that would stay on the head in the strongest breeze were deemed just as important as lace frills and feathers.

The lady in the fur jacket and fancy headpiece (above) looks dubiously at a buggy-type horseless carriage at the first automobile show in 1900. At left, four plumed and furry co-eds of the year 1902 whoop it up for the home team.

*Automobile* magazine in 1908 insisted that the "real season for automobiling" began in September, and displayed these fall styles for female motorists. The lady at top, left, wears a "striped silk rubberized auto coat with auto silk veil." The lady in the center wears a full-length slicker and rain hat to repel September showers, and on the right an English tweed with a high collar is recommended for "cold evening drivers." The lady at bottom, left, displays a huge dust-protecting veil to cover the face and just about everything else, while the lady on the right wears a simple hip-length sweater.

## The "Duster"

No number of hatpins would keep the broad-brimmed ladies' hats of the early days in place in a car devoid of top, windshield, and modern springs. Consequently the scarf or veil tied around the hat and fastened securely under the chin became a necessity. Since paved highways did not supplant dirt roads until after World War I, a ladies' garment appropriately named "the duster" (below) was much in fashion. If rain changed the dust to mud, the neck-to-ankle "duster" was the best protection against mud also. For obvious reasons this popular coat was of hue generally described as "dust-colored." The lady with the feather (lower, right) is out, *sans* protective garb, for what we hope was a short drive.

IN 1908 the Holsman Auto Company (left) called themselves the "oldest motor-buggy makers in America" and refused to let the word "carriage" slip out of their advertising

vocabulary. In rural districts where roads were bad and where high centers were common, the high-wheeled buggy-type automobile seemed destined to survive. Roads and highways improved, however, dirt paths with ruts and high centers gave way to hard composition surfaces, and the high-wheeler faded away into the past. Note also that the Holsman Company announces with justifiable pride that its cars placed first and second in the "greatest hill climbing event in America."

In 1909 open-top Rapid sight-seeing busses sometimes held as many as 30 persons. The Rapid bus at lower left was used for sight-seeing trips in Denver, Colorado. It was equipped with solid tires, folding running boards, and a megaphone carried nonchalantly on the emergency brake lever.

The Davidson-Cadillac Semi-Armored Car (lower right) mounted two guns with armor and had a four-man crew.

## Facts and Blarney, 1909

Since time immemorial there have been two types of advertising: one is a crisp and categorical statement of fact and the other is a ten-ton truck full of blarney. Here is an excellent example of each type. The 1909 McCue Car advertisement is absolutely devoid of adjectives, superlatives, slogans, fancy claims, or propaganda of any variety. It announces the name—The McCue Car—and mentions the weight-horsepower ratio . . . The Oakland ad (below) is a horse of a different color. It starts out with a slogan: "The Oakland is the answer to the man who says 'Show me'." The slogan is immediately followed by a well-rehearsed little routine which starts out, "It is a good old-fashioned American habit, whether buying a cigar or a ten-thousand-dollar house, to look into things a little before spending your money . . ." The reader is halfway through the ad before something specific about the Oakland—its 40-horsepower motor—is mentioned.

### The

### McCue Car

**Sixty-Seven Pounds Weight to the Horse Power**

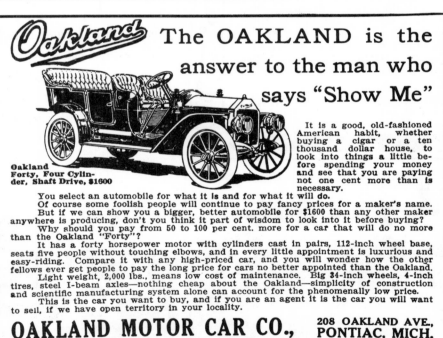

The OAKLAND is the answer to the man who says "Show Me"

Oakland Forty, Four Cylinder, Shaft Drive, $1600

It is a good, old-fashioned American habit, whether buying a cigar or a ten thousand dollar house, to look into things a little before spending your money and see that you are paying not one cent more than is necessary.

You select an automobile for what it is and for what it will do.

Of course some foolish people will continue to pay fancy prices for a maker's name. But if we can show you a bigger, better automobile for $1600 than any other maker anywhere is producing, don't you think it part of wisdom to look into it before buying?

Why should you pay from 50 to 100 per cent. more for a car that will do no more than the Oakland "Forty"?

It has a forty horsepower motor with cylinders cast in pairs, 112-inch wheel base, seats five people without touching elbows, and in every little appointment is luxurious and easy-riding. Compare it with any high-priced car, and you will wonder how the other fellows ever get people to pay the long price for cars no better appointed than the Oakland.

Light weight, 2,000 lbs., means low cost of maintenance. Big 34-inch wheels, 4-inch tires, steel I-beam axles—nothing cheap about the Oakland—simplicity of construction and scientific manufacturing system alone can account for the phenomenally low price.

This is the car you want to buy, and if you are an agent it is the car you will want to sell, if we have open territory in your locality.

**OAKLAND MOTOR CAR CO.,** 208 OAKLAND AVE., PONTIAC, MICH.

Member of the American Motor Car Manufacturers' Association

Will exhibit in New York only at Grand Central Palace Auto Show, opening December 31st.

It is difficult to fathom the purpose and function of some of these 1909 motorcar accessories. For the most part they seem to be bags to put things in and handles for clinging purposes. The bottle opener on the lower right is also a Prest-O-Lite key. Mr. Gilbert manufactured everything from wearing apparel to tire casings, and his products were popular.

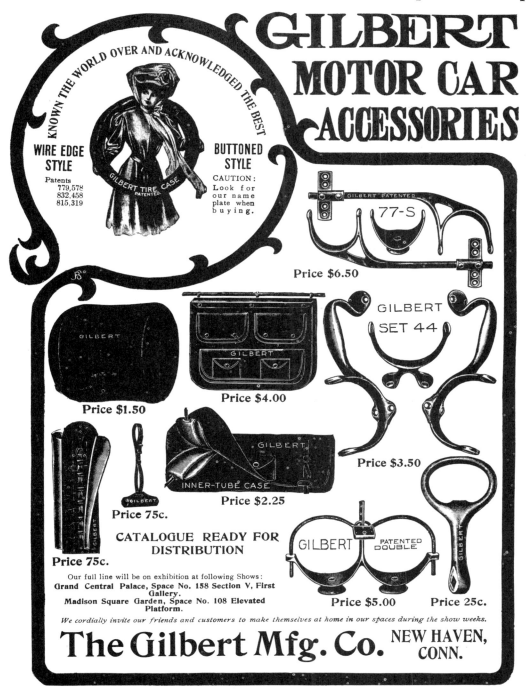

85

## The Steam Car Fades, 1909

The little car below is a 1909 Hupmobile with four cylinders, 20 horsepower, and a $750 price tag. Its slogan was a famous one of the day: "The smartest and best little car ever marketed in America at anything like the money." One of the first bad years for the steam car was 1909. The White Company, and many others, saw the handwriting on the wall and began to manufacture a gasoline model (below, middle) as well as a steam car. They manufactured both steam and gas cars for three years before dropping the steamer. The 1909 Overland Roadster (bottom photo) had a four-cylinder engine and a two-speed planetary transmission.

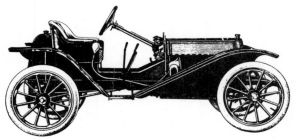

The International Auto Buggy (top) clung to its buggy design even in 1909, insisting that high carriage wheels and solid tires were ageless attributes of any good automobile. Beneath the Auto Buggy, the 1909 Studebaker ($5,100) looks new and glamorous. Glass had finally found its way into car windows, and passengers had their first real protection against the elements. Side curtains rolled down to protect the driver. The car had two sets of lights,

gaslights in front and oil side lamps. Although the top was still made of leather, this 1909 Studebaker, with its metal doorframes and supporting structure, was a close cousin of the all-steel, enclosed bodies that followed. The 1909 Colburn (bottom), built in Denver, was patterned after the French Renault, with the radiator behind the hood.

## *A Sharp Arrow Racer, 1909*

A lot happened in the car world in 1909 and 1910. Ammeters appeared on dashboards that year and the American-La France Company introduced their motor-powered fire wagon. The Neverout Company (below) sold license brackets to those who were nervous about losing their plates and implied in their advertisement that the only way to "avoid arrest" was to buy this gadget first thing in the morning. The Sharp Arrow (bottom), driven by Mr. Sharp himself, proved the big surprise of the Vanderbilt Cup Race in 1909, beating the second car in its class by 50 minutes and averaging almost a mile a minute for 188 miles.

Avoid arrest!
light your
tag this way—
as the law
requires

PENNA 1910
4480

# THE "SHARP ARROW'S"

## SUSTAINED SPEED RECORD
### Averaging a Mile in 1 Minute, 4 Seconds for 188 Miles

An ACKNOWLEDGED AUTOMOBILE ACHIEVEMENT *sui generis*, the fastest time yet made by an American-built machine, declared by press reports to be "the one big surprise of the race," and "the sensation of the races,"—the Vanderbilt Motor Parkway Sweepstake Races—WAS NOT AN ACCIDENT.

The Garden City event was won on merit by the steady, consistent road work of "SHARP ARROW." One news account said: "This car went along at a sixty-mile rate until Mr. Sharp saw that he was distancing his field and took it easy." It was in reality a marvelous feat. "SHARP ARROW" made a new sustained speed record for American cars on its first attempt, beating the next best car in its own class by 50 minutes, beating the entire class above by 15 minutes, and beating all but the two fastest foreign cars, the ISOTTA and RENAULT, in the highest class, cars selling for over $4,000. No wonder that the amazed contestants protested the car, and claimed that it was out of its class—"a car with $6,000 machinery in a cheap body." It certainly behaved like a high-priced machine, and kept the pace set by the fastest company with comparative ease. BUT here are—

The Identical Specifications (plus the Personality of Wm. H. Sharp) of the 1908 "Sharp Arrow" that won the Garden City Sweepstakes, and of every 1909 car that we shall put out:

Mr. F. O. Stanley, who with his bearded twin brother, F. E., invented the Stanley Steamer, is shown below, left, pointing to the boiler of his 1910 precondenser model. This photo was taken in Estes Park, Colorado, where Mr. Stanley lived for many years prior to his death in 1940 and where he built the Stanley Hotel.

The Apperson "Jack Rabbit" (below, right) built in Kokomo, Indiana, was a popular and sporty car in its day, and this 1909 model attracted those interested in speed with a 75-mile-per-hour maximum.

In 1907 tourists to Estes Park were transported in an imposing fleet of Stanley Steamers (bottom). The boy in the front seat of the leading car is the author. These cars replaced the horse-drawn stagecoaches and later on were replaced by busses.

## The Sears Roebuck Car

Few people remember that Sears, Roebuck and Company was once in the automobile business. The Sears car was built in nine models from 1905 to 1910 by the Lincoln Motor Car Works in Chicago. It was meant for the low-price market, its price ranging between $325 and $475. The Sears slogan was "Lowest in Original Cost—Lowest in Upkeep Cost" and their sales policy was perhaps the most lenient in automobile history. They actually sold their cars on ten-day trial.

90

Ten times the price of the Sears, Roebuck car was this 1910 American, "A Car for the Discriminating Few," with the accent obviously on snob appeal. In an attempt to secure a lower center of gravity, a few makes, like the American, were "underslung" by having the frame extend below the axles. This design, according to the ad, gave the automobile a "low and racy appearance." Note the high 40-inch wheels with pneumatic tires and the then-new detachable rims.

# THE AMERICAN

## "A Car for the Discriminating Few"

**The Traveler, 50 H. P., 40-Inch Wheels, $4,250**

Every automobile dealer—every ambitious, wide-awake man who aspires to be a prosperous automobile dealer, will find this page the most important one in THE AUTOMOBILE.

The American's list of agents is to be increased. We are now considering applications from a wide range of cities. There is still time for us to consider your application before our final decision as to allotments of cars for 1911.

Until the close of the 1910 season the outlet for all our cars was made through a few of the larger cities. Buyers were not lacking elsewhere—we simply couldn't get ahead of the demand in those cities with our plant's capacity.

We have greatly increased our manufacturing facilities, because we have conclusively proved that there are buyers everywhere—most desirable buyers—who will have no car but the American if that can be had.

The American is not only a splendid buy from the ordinary viewpoint, but it is—at every speed—*the safest car in the world*, because of its underslung construction. Its ample power, its absolutely straight line drive and its high wheels make it the easiest riding car produced, while it lacks nothing in superb appearance or outward equipment.

There is still time, we repeat, for you to place your application for an American agency. But not much time. You will be wise to write to-day concerning your own city.

Among the 1911 American models, the following types are conspicuous favorites:

| | | | | | |
|---|---|---|---|---|---|
| Traveler | $4,250 | Roadster | $4,250 | Tourist | $4,250 |
| Traveler Special | 5,000 | Roadster Special | 5,000 | Limousine | 5,250 |

## American Motor Car Co. <sub>Dept. E</sub> Indianapolis, Ind.

*Licensed under Selden Patent*

## The Velie, 1910

The August, 1910, issue of the *Horseless Age* carried this full-page advertisement of the Velie 40. This was the beginning of the age of the conveyer belt and the assembly line but complete specialization had not as yet set in. Notice that the Velie ad boasts that "we produce every important part that goes into the Velie 40."

## The Climax in Auto Value

HERE is the one car that combines at a reasonable price every advantage found in cars ranging from $2,500 to $5,000 The Velie 40 is the result of a determination to produce the best possible car at the lowest possible price.

This purpose has been accomplished by reason of extensive manufacturing experience, unlimited capital and the ability to combine purchases for all the affiliated concerns with which the men behind the Velie 40 are connected.

The Velie 40 is made—*not assembled*—by our own workmen in our own factory which is one of the largest, most completely equipped in America.

We produce every important part that goes into the Velie 40 with exception of transmission, steering gear and axles. We would make these if we could improve our car by doing so.

We use Brown-Lipe transmission—the best that mechanical skill can produce or money can buy.

We use the Gemmer steering gear—an exact duplicate of that in the famous Fiat.

We use Timken Roller Bearing axles of special Velie design. Manufacturers who make their own axles cannot excel these.

Our rear axles are chrome nickel steel of a strength which engineers tell us would stand 60 h. p. stress instead of 40 h. p. You will not find such axles on any other $1800 car. At a conservative estimate, 50% of auto troubles are due to defective rear axles. Therefore, 50% of average trouble is absolutely avoided in the Velie 40.

We challenge comparison between the finish of the Velie 40 and that of any car made, regardless of price.

No detail is slighted. This was the policy that brought fame and success to the Deere implement organizations with which we are affiliated. It is bringing fame and success to the Velie 40 likewise.

### SPECIFICATIONS FOR 1911

MOTOR—Bore 4½ in.; stroke 5¼ in., 4 cylinder, 4 cycle **L** type; cylinders cast in pairs with integral water jackets, crank shaft offset ⅜ of an inch. Latest improved foreign design of large bearing roller tappets.

TRANSMISSION—Brown-Lipe selective sliding gear, three speeds forward and one reverse, mounted on four sets of Timken short series roller bearings, designed and manufactured especially for us. Gears 3½ per cent nickel steel.

DIFFERENTIAL—Brown-Lipe bevel gear on Timken roller bearings. Gears of Chrome Nickel steel.

FRONT AXLE—I beam single piece, heat treated drop forging, of Timken manufacture. Wheels on Timken roller bearings.

REAR AXLE—Timken full floating type, double rod construction.

CLUTCH—Dry disc. All parts readily accessible, and replacement costs a minimum.

IGNITION—Splitdorf magneto, with non-vibrating coil as the primary and Atwater Kent for secondary.

LUBRICATION—By gear pump; gear driven. Our patent sight feed is a feature found on no other car. All moving parts and bearings are provided with compression cups or spring oilers.

BRAKES—Double contracting foot brakes and double expanding hand brakes.

SPRINGS—Front semi-eliptic, 38 in. long, 2 in. wide. Rear ¾ in. scroll; 46 in. long and 2 in. wide.

RADIATOR—Mercedes type with hard rubber filler cap.

WHEEL BASE—115 inches. Gear ratio 3 to 1; 3½ to 1.

WHEELS—34 in. artillery type, selected second growth hickory.

TIRES—Hartford or Firestone, 34x4 in. on Hartford Q. D. rims.

STEERING GEARS—Of Gemmer Manufacture.

STEERING WHEEL—Hard Rubber with corrugated finger grips: 17 inches in diameter.

COOLING—By gear driven centrifugal pump.

### A SPLENDID PROPOSITION TO DEALERS

Write at once for particulars of our offer to agents. If you knew as much about the Velie 40 as we do, you would not handle any other car. Let us give you facts. Get in touch with us today.

## VELIE MOTOR VEHICLE CO.
### MOLINE, ILLINOIS

The 1910 Maytag was not only "The Hill Climber" but also "the only whirlwind on wheels." This car was apparently very successful in the racing competition, the hill-climbing contests, the endurance runs, and the speed tests of its day, for the company issued a catalogue highlighting the various records, cups, medals, and trophies that the car had won.

# THE "MAYTAG" Formerly The Mason

## "The Hill Climber"

**This irresistible Car has Whipped them All in Climbing Hills, Endurance, all Displays of Power and Economy of Maintenance.**

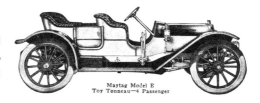

Maytag Model E
Toy Tonneau—4 Passenger

The "Maytag" (formerly the Mason), though of modest price, has been creating sensations in different parts of the country for the past four years.

Climbing hills that are absolutely inaccessible to other cars—winning over cars in the $5,000 class in Glidden tours, hill climbing contests, endurance runs, and the like. See catalog for records, medals, trophies and cups won.

And the Maytag is equally far ahead of all low or medium priced cars in other respects—easiest riding, simplest in operation, most economical in maintenance, travels from four to forty miles an hour on high, and is as silent as a ghost.

Made in six models, $1,250 to $1,750.

Double opposed horizontal and four cylinder—

24 to 28 and 35 to 38 H. P.

*Write for catalog and name of nearest dealer*

For dealers the "Maytag" line for 1910 is the only whirlwind on wheels. Write at once for proposition.

**MAYTAG-MASON MOTOR CO.,** MAYTAG STATION 25 **Waterloo, Iowa**

---

# 1910 *Paterson* "30" $1400

4-Cylinder    30 Horse Power

Write for Agency Proposition

**W. A. PATERSON COMPANY**

FLINT,    MICH.

---

# DARBY

**SIMPLEST AUTOMOBILE ON EARTH**

Simplicity is the keynote of reliability. Simplicity is the Darby's first characteristic. It is simple, staunch and durable. It gives no trouble, but it spins over the road like a monster touring car, or it dodges around the city corners like a bicycle. Let us tell you more about this remarkable car. Send for full descriptive catalog.

**DARBY MOTOR CAR CO.**
536 D. Baliviere Ave.
ST. LOUIS, MO.

**$800**

---

# *Dorris* PRICE $2500

INCLUDING

TOP
TOOLS
SPEEDOMETER

WIND SHIELD
PREST-O-LITE TANK
TIRE IRONS

Licensed under Selden Patents

**DORRIS MOTOR CAR CO., St. Louis, Mo.**

---

# MIDLAND

## 1910

MODEL L—4-40

## Unusual Cars At Common Prices

Big Power, Big Tires, Big Cars—each model of the Midland is a leader in its respective class.

**Model L**—40 Horse Power, Cylinders 4½ in. x 5 in. Wheel base 115 in., Tires 34 in. x 4 in., Toy Tonneau or Roadster with Trunk.

**Model K**—50 Horse Power, Cylinders 4½ in. x 5½ in. Wheel base 118 in., Tires 36 in. x 4 in., Touring Car or Demi Tonneau. Write for free booklet.

**MIDLAND MOTOR CO.** (12) **MOLINE, ILLINOIS**

Licensed Under Selden Patent.

## A Car "Made to Order," 1911

The "Made to Order" phrase in this 1911 Springfield ad is suspect. The specifications are too detailed for a car not as yet made. The companies that made cars for the select "300 exacting people" and defied the laws of mass production, specialization, and low overhead, eventually fell by the wayside.

### The Springfield

### The "Made-to-Order" Car for 300 Exacting People

We will only build 300 "made-to-order" Springfield cars this year. Yet that is three times as many as formerly.

Dealers who desire to supply particular buyers—men who want an unusual car of the "made-to-order" type at $2500—will have an excellent opportunity to do so with these cars. There are a very few choice territories open—write for information.

Built also in Touring Car style as well as Torpedo Body shown here.

### Judge the Springfield by These Specifications:

Motor: 4 cylinder, vertical, water cooled, 5" bore, 4¾" stroke.
Valves: All on one side, interchangeable, operated by single cam shaft with cams integral with shaft and mounted on Annular Ball Bearings, Idler Gear, Pump and Magneto Shaft mounted on genuine imported Annular Ball Bearings.
Transmissions: Selective type, sliding gear, three speeds forward and reverse, mounted on genuine imported F. & S. annular ball bearings. All gears and shafts of heat-treated Chrome Vanadium Steel.
Rear Axles: One-piece seamless drawn Chrome Vanadium Steel housing of the clutch driven floating type. Gears and shaft Chrome Vanadium Steel heat-treated, mounted on genuine imported annular ball bearings.
Front Axles: Special I-beam forged in one piece of heat-treated Chrome Vanadium Steel with ball bearings, steering knuckle.
Frame: Pressed Steel, reinforced.
Springs: Vanadium Steel, semi-elliptic front, three-quarter elliptic rear.
Ignition: Jump spark, 4-unit coil on dash, storage battery, double system with genuine Type D-4 Bosch Magneto, two spark plugs in each cylinder.
Lubrication: Positive, automatic oil system inclosed in crank case of motor.
Drive: Shaft, with large bevel gears of heat-treated Chrome Vanadium Steel.

Brakes: Two independent systems, internal expanding type, Raybestos faced. Foot brake 14" in diameter, operated by cam arrangement.
Body: Straight line, five or seven passengers, sheet metal and upholstered in genuine hand-buffed leather.
Tires: 36 x 5" rear, 36 x 4" front, quick detachable rims.
Steering Gear: Irreversible, 18" wheel, controlling mechanism on top of wheel.
Gasoline Capacity: Twenty gallons under front seat.
Muffler: Our own construction, free and silent, with no back pressure.
Radiator: Latest design genuine honeycomb type, very large and very efficient.
Carburetor: Stromberg, float feed type, auxiliary air valve and water-jacketed.
Clutch: Large cone type with ball thrust bearings, simple means of spring adjustment.
Wheel Base: 128".
Thread: 56½".
Gear Ratio: 3:1.
Clearance: 10".
Color: Green, grays, blues, maroons, yellows, etc.
Weight: 2900 lbs.
Equipment: Top, 2 gas and 3 oil lamps, generator, horn, jack, tire and repair tools.
Price: $2500, Touring or Torpedo Body.

### THE SPRINGFIELD MOTOR CAR CO.,

306 Monroe St.                      Springfield, Ill.

This Amplex "valveless" ad illustrates only one of the many technical controversies that made the growing automobile world exciting and challenging in 1911. Other debates included the two-cycle *versus* the four-cycle engine, the friction transmission *versus* the planetary and sliding gear, air brakes *versus* friction brakes, etc.

# At every point where valves mean expense and waste, no valves mean saving and gain

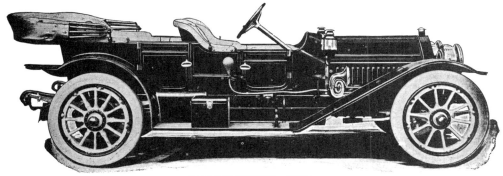

**30-50 TOY TONNEAU. $4,300**

*Amplex*

## Valveless—Self-Starting

It is an interesting truth that the Valveless Amplex counts among its warmest friends and advocates many men who—before they looked into the merits of this car—were deeply prejudiced against a motor without valves.

Seeking an explanation for such a complete reversal of opinion and feeling would reveal the fact that it is due to comparison.

The men who formerly believed their cars which depended upon valves to represent the highest type of motor development and efficiency knew full well the shortcomings and failings of these cars.

More often than was convenient it was necessary to lay up the cars for the grinding of the valves; or the adjustment of valves; or the repair of valves; or the timing of valves; or the removal of carbon deposits from valves and cylinders.

Nor was this all. The more closely observant knew that their cars were rarely, if ever, in the prime condition that assured no loss of power, and no waste of fuel.

Now, happily free from all such vexations and extraordinary expense, these men appreciate and value more highly the splendid car which has shown them the way out—the Valveless Amplex.

They now drive cars that have no valve troubles, because they have no valves; that do not lose power, because they have no valves; that actually produce more pulling power, deliver it continuously, throttle down more closely and pick up more quickly than the finest and smoothest six—because they have no valves.

It is altogether possible that the only thing that prevents your changing to the Valveless Amplex is lack of information about the car.

By all means, if you desire a car of the highest possible sustained efficiency, take steps to inform yourself about the Valveless Amplex.

We are well represented, but if it is inconvenient for you to get in touch with one of our dealers, we shall be glad to send you the catalog and other literature.

# Simplex Motor Car Company
**Mishawaka,**      DEPT. B      **Indiana**

95

# They Hated the Automobile

It is a peaceful summer morning in the year 1901. A horse stands sleepily at a hitching post in front of the general store. In half-hearted fashion he twitches his ears and swishes his tail just to keep the flies moving. Mrs. O'Leary's ten-year-old twin boys are playing marbles at the curb. An occasional wagon rattles by with the reassuring clop-clop of the horse's hoofs on the dirt road.

Suddenly the stillness is shattered by an explosion. Then another, and a third. A hissing, snorting, shivering, black and greasy apparition trundles down the street. A monstrous metal spider! A dragon, no less! Mrs. O'Leary's twins leap from the curb and run shrieking for the house. Doors slam; shades are pulled; Aunt Sadie faints dead away on the chaise longue; and Grandpa reaches for his Winchester.

The automobile had arrived on the American scene.

Early car enthusiasts met with a great deal of opposition and antagonism. The first automobiles terrorized horses, spattered pedestrians with grease and oil, and shook with their vibrations. Whether rightly or wrongly, Mr. Average Conservative in the first decade of the twentieth century was inclined to think that horseless carriages belong on race tracks (upper right) where the drivers could only kill each other and not innocent bystanders. This animosity expressed itself in many ways: threats, violence, legislation, cartoons, and poems. The poetic warning on the right, redundant but effective, is from an early *New York American*.

96

Where They Belong.

### THERE WAS A MAN—BUT THERE ISN'T ANY MORE

There was a man who fancied that by driving good and fast
He'd get his car across the track before the train came past,
He'd missed the engine by an inch, and make the train
    hands sore.
There was a man who fancied this; there isn't any more.

There was a man who thought that he could win a little bet.
By quenching in some gasoline a lighted cigarette.
He thought the fluid, being wet, would douse the flame
    somehow.
There was a man who reasoned thus. He is not with us now.

There was a man, once on a time, who confidently swore
That he'd jump off the Brooklyn Bridge and calmly swim
    to shore.
He said the thrill that he would get would prove extremely
    pleasant.
There was a man who held these views. There isn't at the
    present.

THE PASSING OF THE HORSE

"Oh, Mr. Swift, this

THE HOUSE BEAUTIFUL
Suggestions for a bedroom for an automobile enthusiast.

is——

so sudden!"

"I'M SORRY, MY DEAR, I CAN'T FIND WHAT'S WRONG. I'M AFRAID YOU'LL HAVE TO WALK."

"WHY, GEORGE! I WOULDN'T ASK THE DOG TO WALK ON ROADS LIKE THESE; YOU'LL HAVE TO PUSH THE THING, THAT'S ALL."

*Life Magazine, 1906.*

## Olds and Buick, 1910

HERE are two General Motors cars still in existence, cars that were a part of founder Durant's gigantic empire—the 1910 Oldsmobile (top) and the 1910 Buick. The Oldsmobile Limited was a six-cylinder touring car, unique in that it had huge 42-inch wheels that allowed the car to clear the bumpiest backwoods roads. The car was so high that two levels of running boards were necessary.

The Buick Model 10 (below) was a smaller car with a four-cylinder overhead valve engine. The price was $1,050, and by 1910 the Buick Company was manufacturing 11,000 of these cars, an amazing figure when you realize that Buick sold his first car on July 1, 1904.

1910 OLDSMOBILE "LIMITED" WITH 42-INCH WHEELS

The 1910 Cadillac (below, top) did much to increase the popularity of American cars abroad. Cadillac had won the famous Dewar Trophy in England because of its precision manufacturing. Four Cadillac single-cylinder cars were dismantled and the parts thoroughly mixed. The four cars were then reassembled from the mixed parts, and with these same cars Cadillac made a perfect mechanical score and won the trophy. Interchangeability of parts, with such implications as easy repairs and mass production, was unknown in Britain until that time. . . . One of the highly esteemed light four-cylinder cars in 1910 was the Hudson Model 20 (below, bottom), with its little "bucket" seat behind.

## The Third Model T

It would be difficult to state categorically what was Henry Ford's greatest contribution to the automobile industry. If you asked three persons, you would probably receive three different answers. One would say his early use of the assembly line. Another would reply, "His $5-a-day wage minimum established long before others even considered such high pay." But it is a sure thing that one of the three would claim that the greatest thing Ford ever did was to build the first Model T, or "Tin Lizzie," back in 1908. Below is the third Model T, built in 1910, a roadster with a bucket seat in back and a gas generator on the running board which supplied acetylene gas for the headlights.

When Henry's son, Edsel, joined the company, Ford was producing 180,000 Model T's a year. In 1927 when Edsel, then head of the organization, discontinued production of the Tin Lizzie, his father's favorite car, 15,000,000 Model T's had been manufactured and sold. The Ford Company produced Model T cars for nineteen years, from 1908 to 1927 inclusive; and it is an indisputable fact that there are more Model T's still running on their own four wheels today than any other automobile of that era.

Prize fighters have always used cars filled with manager and cronies for pacing purposes while doing roadwork. In the early days, automobile concerns made advertising capital out of such photographs as (right) the two great heavyweights James J. Jeffries and Jack Johnson being paced in their roadwork by White Steamers before their memorable fight in 1910. Jeffries runs with his manager (top) and Johnson alone (bottom). The photographer, aware of the advertising possibilities, saw to it that no one was standing in front of the prominent "White" on the radiators of the cars when the pictures were taken.

The goal of many car manufacturers was to produce a car that was clean and easy enough for a woman to drive. Many of the early cars were messy and dirty and most women refused to learn to drive. However, Mrs. A. H. Elliott (below) of Alameda County, California, was a skilled driver of her 1910 White Steamer.

## The Parry and the White, 1910

**"IN THE LONG RUN A PARRY"**
*The Parry Idea.*

❡ Away in a Parry!  The sun warms you, the air cleans you.  Sing to the rhythm of your powerful motor while the open road glides beneath. It thrills you to the funny bone.  In the spring a Parry is as irresistible as gravitation.

The Parry ad on the left cannot help but remind one of the Glidden Tours and the influence they exerted on the American public to get out in the wide open spaces and, according to the Parry advertisement, "sing to the rhythm of your powerful motor while the open road glides beneath. It thrills you to the funny bone. In the spring a Parry is as irresistible as gravitation." Once upon a time all automobile manufacturers felt sure that the right poem would sell their cars for them. Verses extolling beautiful buds and Buicks and green grass and Kissel Kars are out of style in the mid-twentieth century, although slogans—"In the Long Run a Parry"—remain with us.

A publicity-conscious 1910 White Steamer, huge and frightening from the front, trails the famous old pedestrian Edward Payson Weston (below) the last day of his transcontinental walk in 1910. Public figures of all kinds made good copy for a still-young product.

The Jackson (below, left), which later developed the famous slogan, "No Hill Too Steep—No Sand Too Deep," was one of the outstanding cars in 1910. The Jackson four-cylinder engine had a unique overhead valve arrangement by which beveled gears operated an overhead camshaft. Most of the fast automobiles built today are constructed on the overhead camshaft principle. The 1910 Rambler Surrey (right, top) had protruding headlights that gave the car a sort of surprised look. It apparently also used the headlights for bumpers. The throttle control on the Rambler was a round disc located directly below the steering wheel. The two-cylinder engine was under the body, and the car was chain-driven.

The Washington ad (below, right) for "The Victor of Victors" features a Greek maiden with wreaths, torch, sword, stars, and flowing robes. The lady seems about to crown the small car for various and sundry victories, too many to mention, in speed, endurance, and hill-climbing contests. This ad, which reached supreme heights in unattractive advertising, also guarantees the car for five years.

103

## Four 1911 Models

The 1911 single-cylinder Brush Runabout had a unique wooden frame, wooden axles, and coil-spring suspension on each wheel. This car was designed by Alanson P. Brush, who also designed engines for the single-cylinder Cadillac and the Oakland car. The engine in the Brush turned counterclockwise, as did the engine in the Oakland, while practically every other automobile engine turned clockwise.

All four of the automobiles advertised below were popular in 1911 and all four of them have since disappeared from the scene. Cole was the last of the four to discontinue, even though founder J. J. Cole still retained his factory.

### Can you afford to be without Everyman's $485
The Brush Runabout Car

WITHOUT a car, you are paying a penalty in time lost, in energy wasted, in healthful recreation missed. You don't need a big, high-powered, high-priced car—expensive to buy and more expensive to run—to enjoy the convenience, the pleasures of an automobile.

The Brush Runabout costs scarcely a cent a mile to run—less than a horse and buggy. It is not only a dependable motor car, but will "earn its keep." It is not a mere pleasure car; it is a "utility" car—a business asset six days of the week, an economical means of recreation outside of office hours.

**The Car for Every Man**

**The business man**—You can get to your office quicker than by street car, cheaper than by train, and the fresh morning air will fit you for the day's work. Then you can keep,

**The farmer**—You can use the Brush in numberless ways—going to town, "getting 'round" the farm, taking produce to market and bringing back the supplies. The women folks can use the car for visiting or shopping, or the children for going to school.

**Any man**—(or employer of men)—whose value depends upon quick transportation, any man who wants to live in the country without being tied to a time table—the Brush is the car you should have.

### ENGER "40" FULLY EQUIPPED $2,000
#### JUST GET OIL AND GASOLINE AND START
The highest type possible in an automobile—fully equipped, without any exception. A few choice territories open. Send for catalog.

**THE ENGER MOTOR CAR CO.** GEST AND SUMMER STS. CINCINNATI, OHIO

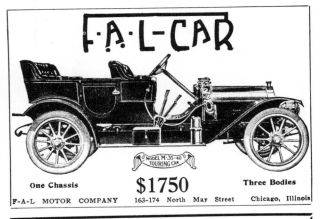

### F-A-L-CAR

Model M-35-40 Touring Car

One Chassis    $1750    Three Bodies

F-A-L MOTOR COMPANY    163-174 North May Street    Chicago, Illinois

### Cole 30—$1500

Don't select your car on a "price tag" basis. Look INTO the car before you look AT the price. Learn what service the CAR will give before you decide what price YOU will give. That is the kind of investigation that sells the Cole "30." One chassis—four bodies.

**COLE MOTOR CAR CO., Makers**
**INDIANAPOLIS, IND.**

Write for Catalog

Torpedo Roadster

Some Territory open for Agencies

### STAVER-CHICAGO

The Staver-Chicago Touring Car at $1,600 and the 5-Passenger Torpedo at $1,850 will give you a decided advantage over your competitor who can only supply their equal at a much higher price.

5-Passenger Torpedo, $1850

**STAVER CARRIAGE COMPANY**
76th and Wallace Streets    CHICAGO, ILL

Motorists before 1910 had to know a lot more about their cars than we do in the mid-20th century. Today we simply watch the meters—when we remember—and run to the gas station when the needle on the dashboard goes above or below the line. It would be strange to have to worry about whether the oil in our cars was circulating properly. Not so in 1908. Many cars then used force-feed oilers, sometimes called sight-feed oilers (below, left), which were usually mounted on the dashboard so that the driver could see the pressure forcing the oil to drop, thus indicating that the oiling system was functioning properly. Most of these oilers had to be regulated with a screw driver.

One of the first expedient car heaters was the collapsible convertible wash basin, which the ingenious motorist filled with hot water and then placed in the general vicinity of his feet. A further refinement was the Clark Auto Heater (below, right) which was popular from 1902 to 1912. In winter weather when heat was desired, charcoal bricks could be heated on a stove and placed in the heater for the car; these charcoal bricks would radiate heat for three to five hours. Many profited by these heaters and some, like Pinocchio, probably burned their wooden legs.

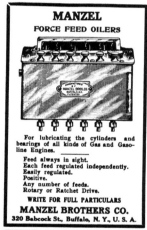

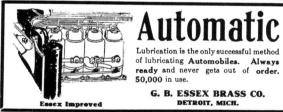

## Barney Came in Second

All kinds of daredevil activities and odd races were once interesting publicity stunts for a young industry. Electric cars raced against men, steam cars against horses, gasoline cars against steam cars, and finally, automobiles against airplanes. In 1911 Lincoln Beachey and his Curtiss Biplane (below), famous for executing the first successful loop-the-loop, defeated the renowned cigar-chomping Barney Oldfield behind the wheel of a racing car in a half-mile contest around a track at San Bernardino, California. . . . The Reo Truck (bottom) carried the baggage, mostly spare tires, for the Glidden Tour in 1911.

BARNEY OLDFIELD.

"BEACHEY WINS"    ©J.I.

A.A.A. GLIDDEN TOUR 1911 BAGGAGE

REO MOTOR TRUCK CO. LANSING MICH.

106

## *Moline and Chalmers, 1911*

When the automobile industry was young, many manufacturers of buggies, plows, tractors, and farm implements (like the Moline Company, top) were induced to jump into the new field, mainly because they already had established sales organizations and retail outlets for their merchandise all over the country. Few of these companies succeeded in their automobile ventures when the competition became tough in later years. Rarely could a company give just part time and a portion of its energy to the booming automobile business and succeed, although International Harvester did.

The 1911 Chalmers (below), "The Car That Won the 1910 Glidden Trophy," believed in factual advertising, no blarney, and high wheels. Note the slogan for the Moline two-seater (above), "The Aristocrat of All Roadsters."

Most of the slogans that made cars famous yesterday are forgotten today. There are exceptions, of course—"Ask the Man Who Owns One" (Packard) or "When Better Cars Are Built, Buick Will Build Them." But who remembers "Perfectly Simple—Simply Perfect" (Maxwell), "An Amazing Car at an Amazing Price" (Overland), or Oldsmobile's "Nothing to Watch but the Road"?

107

# The Indianapolis Speedway

OF all the automobile race tracks throughout the world, none is so famous as the Indianapolis Speedway. Carl G. Fisher, an Indianapolis automobile dealer and part owner of the Prest-O-Lite Company, and three other men who were at the time intensely interested in the development of the automobile built the Speedway in 1909. The others were A. C. Newby, president of the National Motor Car Company, builders of the National automobile in Indianapolis; F. H. Wheeler, manufacturer of the then popular Wheeler-Schebler carburetor; and James A. Allison, a partner of Fisher in the Prest-O-Lite Company.

Indianapolis was then a center of the fast-growing automobile industry, and these gentlemen were eager to do anything to improve and advertise the automobile. It was their opinion that long-distance automobile racing would do more than anything else to improve the design and construction of American cars.

Many people have the idea that the Indianapolis Speedway opened in 1911, when the first 500-mile race was held on Memorial Day. However, the track was built in 1909, and in that same year the first race was won by Robert (Wild Bob) Burman in a Buick. It was a 250-mile race, and the winner's time was 4 hours, 38 minutes, 57 seconds—comparatively slow because of the many accidents that marred the race. The first program was a three-day affair, and owing to the newness of the track there were a number of mishaps. As a result the track was closed and additional work done on it, including the paving of the entire surface with bricks. The last brick was laid in a suitable ceremony by Governor Tom Marshall of Indiana, the man who later became Vice-president but was even more famous for his remark, "What this country needs is a good 5-cent cigar."

The next meeting on the Indianapolis Speedway was held on December 18, 1909, in extremely cold weather. The most notable race was won in a 120-horsepower Fiat by a driver named Strang who covered 5 miles in 3 minutes, 17 seconds to establish a new record and beat the former record for that distance held by the renowned Barney Oldfield.

There were many events held at Indianapolis in 1910, but the first 500-mile event was held on May 30, 1911, and won by Ray Harroun in a Marmon Wasp. Harroun led for more than 300 miles but at no time was very far in advance of his rivals. He covered the distance in 6 hours, 42 minutes, and won $10,000 first place; in second place was the famous early-day driver, Ralph Mulford, in a Lozier; and third place went to David Bruce-Brown.

The second 500-mile race, in 1912, was won by Joe Dawson, driving a National with an average speed of 78.72 miles an hour. Ralph DePalma in a Mercedes was leading when he was eliminated 5 miles from the finish. With victory in sight, a broken piston put DePalma out of the running. Even then he did not give up hope of winning, for he and his mechanic, Rupert Jeffkins, jumped out of the machine and desperately pushed it along the track.

From 1913 to 1920 European drivers, who came over in large numbers, showed that the Old World had superior machines. An American-made car did not win again until Gaston Chevrolet in a Monroe won in 1920. In 1913 an excitable little Frenchman by the name of Jules Goux, driving a French Peugeot, won $20,000 first prize, averaging 75.92 miles per hour. 1914 was an all-French victory. René Thomas, driving a Delage, won first place; another French Peugeot driven by Duray was second; Guyot, driving a Delage, was third; and the 1913 winner Goux placed fourth, again in a Peugeot.

In 1915 another foreign-built car, a German Mercedes, won first place when its driver, Ralph DePalma, averaged 89.84 miles per hour. Dario Resta, an Italian, driving a Peugeot, won second place. In 1916 the Italian driver Resta, again driving a Peugeot, won first place, with D'Alene in a Duesenberg second and Mulford in a Peugeot third. The average was 84.05 miles per hour. During the war years of 1917 and 1918 there were no races. They were continued again in 1919, when Howard Wilcox, driving a Peugeot, came in first, with Hearne in a Durant placing second and Jules Goux in a Peugeot, third.

In 1920 Gaston Chevrolet, driving an American-built Monroe, finished in first place in the first car built in the United States to win the Indianapolis classic since 1912. Chevrolet averaged 88.16 miles per hour. René Thomas in a French Ballot was second, and Tommy Milton in a Duesenberg was third. . . . Inasmuch as this book deals for the most part with automotive history prior to the twenties, no further Indianapolis results are included. Ray Harroun (below), winner of the 500-mile race in 1911, is pictured in the Marmon Wasp.

**LOZIER WINS ANOTHER VICTORY**

**WORLDS RECORDS BROKEN**

On March 19th
Teddy Tetzlaff with a
46 H. P. Lozier stock car.
defeated Ralph De Palma with
his 90 H. P. imported Grand Prize Fiat
racing car in a 100 mile match race on
the 1 mile Los Angeles Motordrome, winning by over 6 miles
and breaking the World's Records from 25 to 100 miles in
the phenomenal average time of 80 55-100 miles per hour.
Time for 100 miles: 1 hour, 14 minutes and 29 seconds.

## These Constant Lozier Victories

have a meaning of deep significance. Tetzlaff's victory over De Palma was the
sixteenth consecutive event in which Lozier stock cars have met and defeated
great cars and great drivers, broken World's Records or won National Champion-
ships. *Yet in all these great events there is not recorded a single instance of a
breakdown or failure to finish*—a succession of perfect performances without a
parallel in the entire history of Automobile Contests. They signify supreme endurance and marvelous mechanical perfection.

## Lozier Cars Are Not Racing Cars

they are beautiful, comfortable cars of character and refinement, raced merely to
demonstrate their wonderful powers of endurance and perfect mechanical construction. No other car is used by so great a number of experienced motorists—
men of experience with other high-class cars of the world—who demand and are
satisfied with nothing less than absolute satisfaction.

Can you afford to overlook a car of this remarkable character?

The agency for the Lozier car is a valuable asset. Correspondence solicited with dealers in unoccupied territory

**LOZIER MOTOR COMPANY,** DETROIT, MICH.
P. O. Box 718

110

THE Lozier was much more than a racing car, although a racer with a Lozier engine won the 1911 Los Angeles Motordome match race and broke a few records doing it (opposite page). The car below, in 1913, was one of America's finest quality automobiles. It was glass-enclosed and could advertise both an electric lighting and an electric starting system. The "Big Six" Lozier had an 88-horsepower engine, and left-hand drive, and sold for $5,000. Notice the unusual single door in the center.

111

## Trancontinental Truck

The year that ex-Princeton Professor Woodrow Wilson, author of the famous "Fourteen Points" and coauthor of the League of Nations, was sent to the White House by a record vote in the Electoral College, the first motor truck crossed the continent under its own power (bottom, left). The year was 1912 and the truck was a Packard which carried a three-ton load all the way. The performance was hailed as a truly remarkable demonstration of endurance and stamina and it introduced a new era of transcontinental trucking. The truck made the trip from New York to San Francisco in 47 days in the hottest part of the summer.

The 1911 Rambler (top, left) was one of many cars once made in the state of Wisconsin. The side view, with the spare tire on the running board, makes the Rambler look at if it were all wheels.

One of the most famous cars advocating the friction drive was the Cartercar (top, right). The Henderson (right, middle) advertised dynamic lights, a self-starter, and "more car for less money." The King Company (lower right) went into the logistics of automobiles and claimed that their "long wheel base . . . gives perfect distribution of the load." Its full equipment also includes a self-starter. By 1911 the crank was fast disappearing—except on the Model T Ford.

*Packard*

The first motor truck to cross the continent entirely under its own power. Left New York July 8th; reached San Francisco August 24th. Carried a 3-ton load all the way.

This is a remarkable demonstration of the stamina and capability of the Packard truck under every conceivable condition of hauling. The trip is one that has been accomplished by only a very few automobiles. The venture has been regarded as virtually out of the question for a heavy truck.

It was easily within the ability of the Packard truck because both Packard trucks and Packard cars are built to surmount difficulties much greater than they encounter in actual service.

Their margin of efficiency is your margin of safety in purchasing Packards for whatever purpose.

The Packard 3-ton truck is used in 137 lines of trade and in 205 cities. Dealers with Packard standard Service Depots in 104 different cities.

*Packard Motor Car Company, Detroit, Michigan*

112

"Spark plugs need cleaning too" is the catch line of an advertisement we see on billboards and in magazines almost every day. Yet who gives a second thought to the years of experimenting and research that contributed to the nearly perfect mechanisms that sit beneath the hoods of our automobiles today? The illustration of well-known makes of spark plugs used in 1911 (below) is interesting because of the various sizes, shapes, types, and designs, many of which do not conform to our conception of what a spark plug should look like. Some makes had priming cups to ease winter starting.

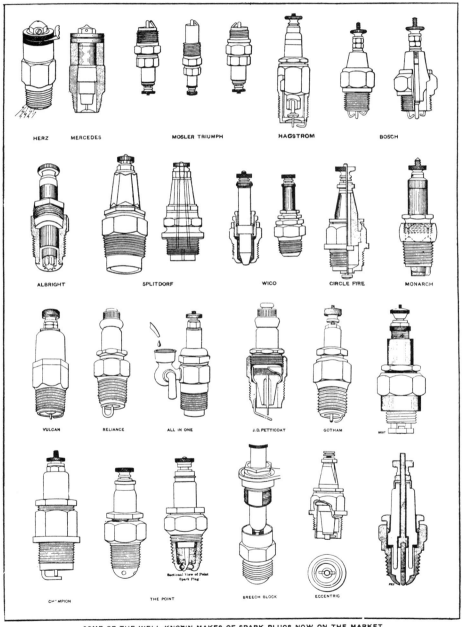

SOME OF THE WELL-KNOWN MAKES OF SPARK PLUGS NOW ON THE MARKET

## Buick, Chevrolet, Cadillac

This 1911 Buick (below, top) was a five-passenger touring car which sold for $1,500 (considerably less than the cheapest Buick sells for today) and advertised the usual three speeds forward and one reverse which were standard in many cars by 1911. Accessories and equipment included oil side-and-rear lamps, gas headlights, generator, horn, foot rest, robe rail, tools, jack, pump, and tire-repair kit. Buick's 1911 production figure of 3,000 of these cars hardly compares favorably with the 180,000 Model T's Henry Ford manufactured in 1912.

The two-tone 1913 Chevrolet (bottom, left) was the second car the company manufactured. In its first year, 1912, Chevrolet produced 2,999 cars, all of the same model, a five-passenger touring car which sold for $2,150. It was not until later that Chevrolet decided to compete for the low-price market. "The Car That Has No Crank" (bottom, right) was the famous Cadillac "30" of 1912. Its formidable electric lights comprised another prime selling feature.

This monstrous-looking vehicle with white-wall tires was probably one of the most radically designed experimental cars ever built in the United States. It was called the Bi-Autogo and was constructed between 1908 and 1912 by a well-known Detroit artist and engineer, James Scripps Booth. It had six wheels—one large one in front and back and two sets of two small ones toward the middle. However, it used only two, like a motorcycle, when in motion. Powered by one of the first V-8 engines, of Booth's own design, it developed 45 horsepower.

Other features were a compressed-air starter, folding armrest, and invisible door hinges. Later, Mr. Booth designed, built, and sold the well-known Scripps-Booth car.

AMERICANS remember the name of Henry Ford (1863–1947). He not only produced the low-priced car for the millions and established the $5 minimum daily wage (almost unbelievable at the time) but he built one of the first great industrial empires. In 1896 while working for the Detroit Electric Company, he built his first car, a small crude two-cylinder automobile. Ford produced many early cars that did not become immediately popular and was hard pressed when his first low-priced $500 Model N car started him on his upward climb.

Ford's first gasoline engine (drawings below) was tested in his kitchen in 1893. The present Ford Motor Company, organized in 1903 and capitalized at $150,000, paid its founder $3,000 the first year. The first factory (below) was a two-story building in Detroit.

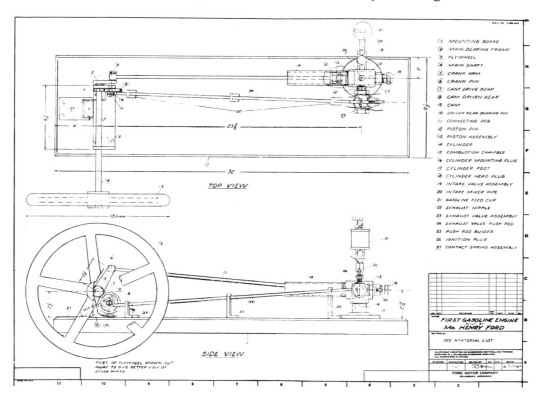

## Ford Started Slowly

Ford's 1904 payroll (below) was on a modest scale and the Model B (below, right) manufactured in 1903, received little recognition. From 1903 to 1911 Ford, with a few others, waged a court fight for the whole automobile industry against the patent of George B. Selden (news clipping, right) who claimed all manufacturers had to pay him royalties through the Association of Licensed Automobile Manufacturers who controlled the Selden Patent.

| | |
|---|---|
| H Ford | 416 62 |
| J Couzens | 166 66 |
| J Wills | 125 00 |
| J H O'Brian | 87 50 |
| Audrich | 80 33 |
| Ch Grant | 6 250 |
| Hayes | 6 250 |
| Kulick | 5000 |
| Carey | 5000 |
| Grose | 3 750 |
| Aikenhead | 50 |
| Limbach | 50 |
| Clarkson mfg | 1750 |
| Contrik | 25 00 |
| L Hauck | 20 |
| H Rockelman | 3 250 |
| Hogue | 50 00 |
| H Liff | 50 |
| Meijer | |
| Miller | 20 00 |
| Mead | 6 250 |
| Lofie | 3 250 |
| Linden CH | 37 50 |
| Kaplan | 25 left |
| Parsons | 50 00 |

In 1904 a merchant of some renown, John Wanamaker, advertised a world speed record made by Ford in his famous Ford "999" racer. Next Ford startled the industry with the exceedingly low price of $500 when he offered his Model N in 1905 (below, top), a light four-cylinder car which sold for less than single-cylinder machines produced by Cadillac, Reo, Rambler, and Oldsmobile. In 1905 he produced a two-cylinder Model C (below, middle) with a detachable rear tonneau. In 1906 and 1907 he experimented with high-priced, heavier

cars when he built the six-cylinder Model K at his new three-story brick factory (bottom photo). After two years he discontinued production of the heavier models, determined to find a mass market with a good but inexpensive automobile. The fruit born of this decision was perhaps America's most famous automobile, the Ford Model T, first manufactured in 1908. Fifteen million Model T's were sold in the following nineteen years. Although Edsel Ford was at the head of the organization in 1928 when the Model A replaced the "T," the destiny of the Ford empire was always managed and controlled by old Henry until a short time before his death on April 7, 1947.

119

## Henry's Empire

Ford's empire was the first of its kind in the automotive trade. He owned coal mines and iron mines and timber tracts. He built steel mills and launched a fleet of freight ships. He bought railroads in Michigan and rubber plantations in Brazil. He constructed whole towns for his employees, built automobile museums, guaranteed his workers an unheard-of daily wage of $5, manufactured three different makes of automobiles, and in 1923 flatly refused to be a candidate for the presidency of the United States. Aside from the 1,100-acre River Rouge Plant and the gigantic engineering laboratories at Dearborn, Michigan, the company operated 27 factory branches, more than a score of hydroelectric plants, and 31 companies on foreign soil. At one time or another the company has made, among other things, tractors, trucks, boats, and all-metal airplanes. Henry Ford was a phenomenon even in the phenomenal age of American industrial expansion.

Ford did much to help develop the assembly line. In 1913 Ford employees tried a new type of line (right, top) in which the body came sliding down from above to be mounted on the chassis. The 1907 six-cylinder Model K (right, second photo) known as the "Gentlemen's Roadster" and sometimes as the "Silent Cyclone," sold for $2,800. The 1907 Model S (right, third photo) was the last model with a steering wheel on the right-hand side. The first Model T two-door sedan (bottom photo) was built in 1915.

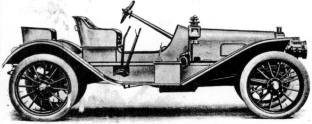

120

IN 1911 Arizona applied for statehood. Court decisions against Standard Oil and tobacco trusts in the spring of that year were the first instances of the dissolution of great industrial combinations. These victories spurred the administration on to a total of 45 indictments of monopolistic concerns, including a sweeping indictment of the United States Steel Corporation. To the automobile trade 1911 was the year the United States Court of Appeals declared the Selden Patent invalid, which meant that car manufacturers were no longer in danger of suits and heavy royalty payments. George B. Selden, the man who built a two-cylinder internal-combustion engine 'way back in 1877, had lost an eight-year patent suit. Also in 1911, Buick produced its first closed car and Cadillac was toying with an electric starter. The car with the spare tire in the back seat (below) is the unusual 1910 Oldsmobile with 42-inch wheels. The Herreshoff Company (top picture), one of the early Detroit outfits, offered a $950 roadster with a single seat in the back, precursor of the now outdated rumble seat.

The 1911 Octoauto had eight wheels and claimed that each tire lasted longer, since it carried one-eighth of the load instead of one-fourth. Modern cars do not adhere to this principle.

# THE OCTOAUTO

## AN APPRECIATION BY ELBERT HUBBARD

¶ In the good old days when I used to take cattle to the Chicago Stock Yards, I carried a long hickory pole, a basket of grub, and much enthusiasm.

¶ On long runs, my home was in the caboose for perhaps three days and three nights. It was a sad day, however, when, instead of a regular, genuine caboose, they bundled the merry stockmen into a dinkey.

¶ The difference between a dinkey and a caboose is that a caboose has four wheels on each side, and a dinkey has only four wheels altogether, one on each corner. The dinkey's business is to bounce, jounce, jolt, jar and jerk, and make a puncture in your vocabulary.

¶ A wheel is a plan of continually hitting the rail. The Pullmans, it was, who discovered that when you hit the rail in twelve places in running a car, you greatly reduce the amount of jar and the wear and tear both on the rails and the rolling-stock.

¶ A car having twelve wheels is considered doubly as safe as one having eight.

¶ A wheel lives its life exactly as a man does his. A man will stand a great number of raps and kicks supplied by Fate, provided they are distributed over a long period of time, but when you come to concentrate them in a few years, or a few months, or a few days, you destroy the man by destroying his nerve fabric.

¶ In the Reeves Octoauto, the load is distributed over eight wheels, instead of being concentrated on four. In a four-wheeled automobile, a wheel at each corner carries one-fourth of the load. In case of an imperfection in the road, the sudden dropping down into a rut, one wheel may for an instant carry half of the load, and it is this sudden jolt and burden that causes the tire trouble. You get enough of these tremendous pressures in a day, and your tire reaches its limit and explodes with a loud R. G. Dun and Company report. If you are running fast, you may lose control and the ditch, always waiting, gets you. So the proposition is, if you can save your wheels from these severe jolts which will occasionally come through dropping into a rut, you are going to prolong the life of the tire, the life of the car and the life of its occupants.

The article by Elbert Hubbard is as unusual and startling as the Octoauto.

¶ When you break your leg or sprain your ankle, it is not on account of long, slow service. It is because you get a sudden twist or smash. Just so with tires—it is jam and jar that does the business.

¶ It is figured out on a reasonable basis that by the use of eight wheels, eight times the ordinary service is obtainable. If a car were always evenly balanced on four wheels, your tires would live probably ten times as long as they now do; but in turning corners and dropping into ruts, and hitting high places, a severe shock has to be met by your wheel. It is the accumulated results of these shocks that lays you up at the inopportune time.

¶ I had the pleasure of riding in an Octoauto in Chicago. The driver was a reckless fellow, and the wonder is that we were not pinched and given the limit by the judge; but fortunately our driver picked streets that no other auto with a sane chauffeur would attempt to navigate.

¶ Chicago not only has some of the best pavement in the world, but I believe it can safely claim the booby-prize for the worst.

¶ The worst pavement possible is the Nicholson Blocks, where time gets the better of their ego. A busted-up Nicholson pavement is absolutely the end of the limit. We took Nicholson pavement, which was laid in Eighteen Hundred Eighty-five, at the rate of twenty-five miles an hour, absolutely oblivious of the ruts. Very few of these ruts were over three feet, but so evenly was the weight divided that we were on terra cotta most of the time, and the wear and tear and jar were distributed, for before one wheel could really go down and hit the bottom of a rut, the wheel behind it was to the rescue on firm footing and relieved the strain. ¶ This taking ruts and bumps without jar is something that no man can possibly appreciate who has not experienced a ride in an Octoauto.

¶ In this thing of running over a surface filled with ruts that are from three to six inches deep, and yet experiencing scarcely any bounce, jounce, jar or jolt, two big items are obtainable. One is ease to the passenger, and the next is, length of life to the auto.

¶ The whole arrangement is very simple and is a shock-absorber beyond the dreams of the neurotic.

¶ THE REEVES "OCTOAUTO" Car is conventional throughout, except the four additional carrying wheels. Steers and controls exactly the same as a four-wheeled car.

¶ The Only Easy-Riding Car in the World.

¶ The only car in the world built on the principle of a Pullman Palace-Car.

¶ The Easiest Car in the World on Tires.

¶ Tire authorities say that tires on an Octoauto should give eight times the ordinary service.

¶ This truly wonderful car is manufactured and sold by

# M. O. REEVES, COLUMBUS, INDIANA

President Peoples Savings and Trust Company, Vice-President Reeves Pulley Company.

who will be glad to send full descriptive pamphlet containing prices to those interested. Agents wanted.

## The Sextoauto

The Sextoauto (below) was built by the company that produced the car with eight wheels, the Octoauto, and again they claimed that their multiwheeled invention rode "like a Pullman and is bound to revolutionize automobile construction where comfort in riding is a consideration." Tire trouble and expense were supposedly going to be reduced because the wear and tear on a tire supporting one-sixth of the car's weight is naturally less than if each wheel shoulders one-quarter of the burden. Some trucks and trailers built today have rear wheels like the Sextoauto's. In 1912 the Pierce-Arrow Company (bottom) of Buffalo advertised "a new type of body with the last traditions of horse-drawn vehicles wholly abandoned." Percy Pierce, of Pierce-Arrow fame, won the Glidden Tour in 1905.

# THE PIERCE-ARROW

## Ten Years' Progress

**1901** 1-CYLINDER 2¾-H. P. MOTORETTE

**1902** 1-CYLINDER 3½-H. P. MOTORETTE

**1903** 2-CYLINDER 15-H. P. TOURING CAR

**1904** 2-CYLINDER 15-H. P. TOURING CAR

**1905** 4-CYLINDER 24-28-H. P. TOURING CAR

RECENTLY there was held in Buffalo, N.Y., an exhibition of Buffalo-made products. One of the features of the week of display was a motor-car parade, in which the Pierce-Arrow Motor Car Company took part. Owners of Pierce-Arrow cars in Buffalo assisted the company in its display of models from 1901 on to the cars manufactured almost on the day of the parade. Seldom has any city witnessed so impressive an exhibition of what has been accomplished in motor-car advancement in a decade as was shown when the Pierce-Arrows of each succeeding year, from the little 2¾-horsepower motorette to the majestic 66-horsepower suburban car of to-day, moved in line together. Those who saw this exposition realized from what their own eyes told them that they were seeing the unfolding of a story that contained illustratfons of the mechanical and artistic efforts of men who had striven for a decade with a single purpose to guide them—the betterment of the Pierce-Arrow.

THE PIERCE-ARROW

MOTOR CAR CO.

BUFFALO, N. Y.

**1906** 4-CYLINDER 28-32 H. P. TOURING CAR

**1907** 4-CYLINDER 40-45 H. P. TOURING CAR

**1908** 6-CYLINDER 40-H. P. TOURING CAR

**1909** 6-CYLINDER 48-H. P. TOURING CAR

**1910** 6-CYLINDER 48-H. P. TOURING CAR

**1911** 6-CYLINDER 48-H. P. TOURING CAR

**1912** 6-CYLINDER 48-H. P. TOURING CAR

*In 1912, Only $7250*

The American Locomotive Company in 1912 produced the Alco car with Pullman ventilators in the roof, upholstery 10 inches deep, and illuminated steps. Price—$7,250!

## ALCO

| | |
|---|---|
| 6-cylinder, 60 H. P. Landaulet | $6750 |
| 6-cylinder, 60 H. P. Limousine | 6750 |
| 6-cylinder, 60 H. P. Berline Limousine | 7250 |
| 4-cylinder, 40 H. P. Landaulet | 5500 |
| 4-cylinder, 40 H. P. Limousine | 5500 |
| 4-cylinder, 40 H. P. Berline Limousine | 6000 |

## A Daring New Berline

HERE is pictured the Alco Berline. It is the latest and newest car in America.

Daring, new lines—new ideas in refinement—a new conception of a motor car.

Note the roof lines—the breaking away from the old, the commonplace, the stereotyped—and in their stead the original, the beautiful.

Observe the Pullman ventilators in the roof. Fresh air, warmth, no drafts.

Wide 25½-inch doors, upholstery 10 inches deep, and a large area of room within.

Steps illuminated at night—automatic by opening the door.

The white stripe around the graceful body—a badge of motor individuality.

These suggest the ultra in the Alco.

Price $7250.

Catalog on request.

**AMERICAN LOCOMOTIVE COMPANY, 1893 Broadway, NEW YORK**

Builders also of Alco Motor Trucks and Alco Taxicabs

Chicago Branch: 2501 Michigan Avenue
Boston Branch; 567 Boylston Street

Canadian Headquarters:
596 St. Catharine Street, W., Montreal

Twice winner of the race for the Vanderbilt Cup

126

The Kissel Motorcar Company refused to state whether their 1912 "semi-touring" model was a four- or five-passenger car. It was "roomy for four but not overcrowded by five."

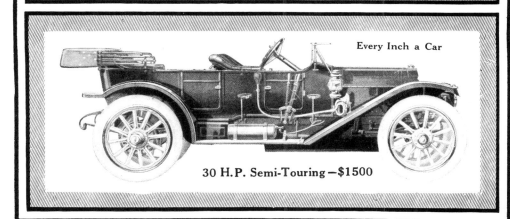

## Electric Headlights

Around 1912, the year the liner *Titanic* sank in the North Atlantic after ramming an iceberg, significant changes in automotive design were taking place. Electric headlights had in many cases replaced the old acetylene generator and Prest-O-Lite tank. The Multiplex Touring Car (top) had both electric headlights and ultramodern flush side lights for a mere $3,600. The more reasonably priced Studebaker-Flanders (below) had the old-fashioned type of illumination: three oil lamps and an acetylene generator for its headlights. It also had a four-cylinder engine and a three-speed transmission mounted on the rear axle and was considered an excellent buy in its day.

To bridge the interval between crank and battery, the Prest-O-Lite Company invented an acetylene-gas starter in 1912 which was operated by a little pump.

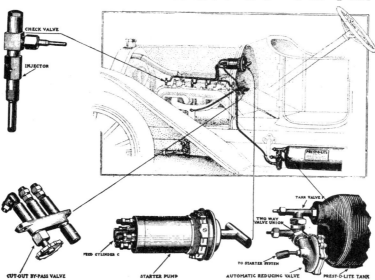

*Everything's Electric, for $5000*

The 1913 Marmon Six was an enormous seven-passenger car which, for $5,000, supplied every type of electrical appliance: starter, dashboard light, step light, and emergency lamp.

## "The Easiest Riding Car In The World"
# The MARMON SIX

*Marmon "48"—(Six)—Seven-Passenger Touring Car—$5000.00*

YOU may know, by a glance, of the Marmon's luxury, its beauty, its completeness of appointment, its fitness to be classed first among the best.

You may know its superiority of design, materials and construction by actual records in the hands of owners and the world's greatest contests.

But a new and different sensation, the realization of true Marmon value, grows as you come to own and admire this car for its adaptability to meet your every requirement with delightful satisfaction.

### Outline Specifications

**Motor**—4½"x6", "T" head, 48-80 h. p. **Oiling**—Marmon system automatic force feed lubrication, delivering oil through hollow crank shaft directly into main bearings, connecting rod bearings and piston pin bearings, also through hollow cam shafts to cam shaft bearings. **Ignition**—Two spark dual system. **Clutch**—Improved dry plate multiple disc. **Rear Axle**—Floating type unit with transmission. Pressed steel housing. **Front Axle**—A new type, an exclusive feature of the Marmon Six. The vertical spindle is placed in the direct center line of the wheel. This construction makes the safest, surest and easiest steering mechanism ever devised. **Brakes**—Internal expanding, 403 sq. in. surface. **Wheelbase**—145 in. **Rims**—Quick detachable, demountable. **Tires**—Front 36x4½, rear 37x5; front and rear rims and tires interchangeable. **Steering Gear**—Left-hand with center control. **Carburetor**—Improved automatic. **Springs**—Front, semi-elliptic; rear, ¾ elliptic. **Body**—Convex curve type Marmon perfected cast aluminum construction with sheet metal seat backs. Deep cushions. Nickel trimmed. **Equipment**—Electric starting and lighting system, cape top, windshield designed as part of dash with provision for ventilation, speedometer and clock, electric light to illuminate entire dash, electric step light under tonneau doors, electric emergency lamp with long extension cord, electric horn, power tire pump, shock absorbers front and rear, tire carrier, extra demountable rim, coat rail, foot rest, assortment of tools, oiler, jack and tire repair kit. **Prices**—Seven, Five, Four or Two-Passenger Body Types, $5000.00; Limousine (seats seven) $6250.00; Berlin Limousine (seats seven) $6450.00; Landaulet (seats seven) $6350.00.

### New England Dealers
**F. E. WING MOTOR CAR COMPANY, "Motor Mart," 12 Columbus Ave., Boston**
Manufactured By
# Nordyke & Marmon Company
**Indianapolis**        (Established 1851)        **Indiana**

## Sixty Years of Successful Manufacturing

Foreign cars had an enviable reputation in 1913, but they were not mass-produced and were therefore expensive. American advertisers used such slogans as the one below.

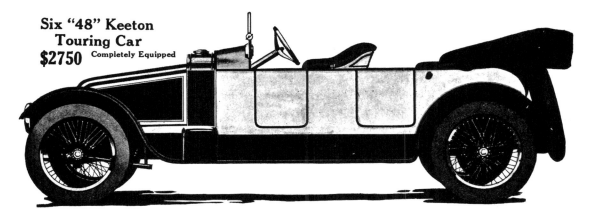

**Six "48" Keeton Touring Car**
**$2750** Completely Equipped

# An European Type—At An American Price!

Few people will deny that they consider foreign cars better in many ways than those made in this country.

They are distinctive and more attractive in design, and have several features of construction which mean more efficient service. But the only fault found is in the price, which is very exorbitant to most buyers, because of the methods employed by the European builders and the high tariff.

Now in the Keeton you have a car that combines the very best ideas both in construction and designing, that have been produced on both continents.

And you buy the Keeton, with these advantages, at the American price.

The Keeton car answers every requirement of those people who want a car of foreign design, yet who feel that they do not want to pay the high prices.

Electric Starting.

Full Electric Light Equipment.

Transmission—four speeds forward.

Wire Wheels—with option of Wood Wheels.

Chrome Vanadium Gears and Shafts on imported Annular Ball Bearings.

Extra Detachable Wire Wheel, or Extra Demountable Rim.

Long easy riding Springs—long wheel base.

Left Hand Drive—Center Control.

Small bore—long stroke motor of exceptional power and flexibility.

Radiator at rear of motor—in proper and protected position.

The only true French type of car built in America.

Best of foreign practice adapted to American road and touring conditions.

## Complete Equipment

Electric starting and lighting system, with 12 1-2-inch head lights; tail lamp with license holder; 80-mile Speedometer and eight-day clock combined with electric light; Lamp for changing tires at night, with extension cord; Dynamo electric Horn; Robe and Foot Rails; Silk Mohair Top, with self-contained folding curtains and slip cover; Double acting rain vision Windshield; Option of Wire Wheels with extra detachable Wire Wheel, or Wood Wheel with extra demountable rim; Wheel or Tire Carrying Irons; Full Set of tools; Pump; Jack and Tire Repair Outfit, and all Touring Bodies will take Auxiliary Seats.

## Three Excellent Models

Riverside Touring Car, 5-passenger, Completely
  Equipped ................................ $2,750
Two extra folding seats for above............  25
Meadowbrook Roadster, Completely Equipped..  2,750
Tuxedo Coupe, Completely Equipped...........  3,000
Chassis without tires or rear guards..........  2,250
All Prices f. o. b. Factory.  Booklet on Request.

**To Dealers:** It is needless for us to say that these cars are selling fast. Nearly two-thirds of our 1913 output has already been sold. And when we say sold we mean contracted and paid for.

This is the one distinct car—the one car that has a demand all its own. It is the one car that has no competition from American cars because of the style and design, and none from the foreign cars because of the price. The Keeton car appeals to the buyer who is accustomed to the best—but who will appreciate a fair price.

The Keeton is selling fast wherever we are showing it. We already have dealers in many localities, and are considering applications from others. It would be well for you to write us about your local territory. We may already have a dealer lined up, but will be glad to hear from you anyway.

# Keeton Motor Co.          Detroit, U. S. A.

Musical horns had a short vogue around 1913, about the time the rubber-bulb horns were being replaced by our modern electric horns. An unmusical horn, claims the Aermore ad on the left, "alarms and unnerves pedestrians and makes them run into danger instead of away from it." On the other hand, if the horn was too musical, the fascinated pedestrian might stand transfixed in the middle of the street and run into trouble that way.

The Boyce Motometer (bottom) was better than guessing at the temperature of your car, but the 1913 designer felt that his instrument had to sit right on top of the radiator cap to record temperatures accurately. Peering the length of the car to read the temperature was hard on the nearsighted motorist, and it was not easy to see it at night.

In 1912 Americans began to notice the expression "trouble in the Balkans" in the newspapers. The same year Louis J. Bergdoll of the well-known Philadelphia Bergdolls offered a wide assortment of models in his Bergdoll "30." The car was assembled by using well-known units such as Westinghouse-made engine, Livingston radiator, Warner transmission, Bosch magneto, and Continental quick demountable rims. A one-year guarantee was a sales argument and "a demonstration could be arranged." The Bergdoll limousine had up-to-the-minute glass windows but honking the horn was still a matter of pressing the bulb.

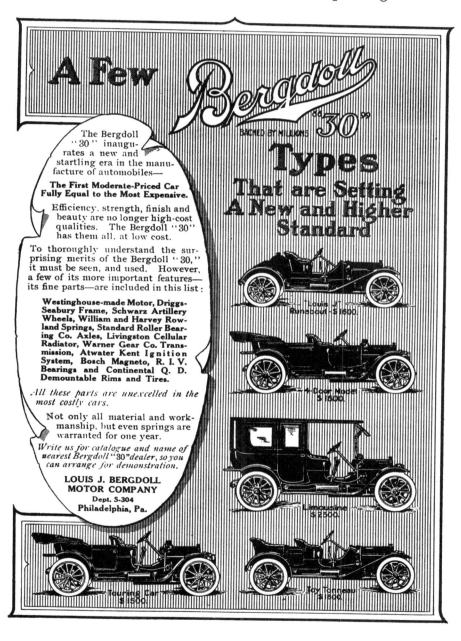

## Back-seat Driver, 1913

In 1913, the year that Packard first developed forced-feed lubrication, the Benham Company produced a six-cylinder, four-speed limousine that sold for $2,585. The Benham Six (top photo) had left-hand drive, center control of the gearshift lever and the hand brake, and electric lights and starter. Skelton and Goodwin, who later became famous designers and engineers, designed the car.

The same year a most unusual car called the Duck was offered to a confused public of car buyers. The Duck, built by Jackson, was unique in that the driver—the original "back-seat driver"—sat in the rear seat and his passengers were carried on folding chairs directly in front of him. The Duck was advertised as something "new, exclusive, individual, different, like no other, and something you will want." It was also billed as "the newest, latest, best thing ever produced in the auto line." All the superlatives in no way explain the advantages of the driver sitting behind his passengers, and the fact that no such dangerous vehicles exist today only vouches for the good sense of the American car buyer. It is interesting to speculate how the rear-seat driver of the Duck fared if his passengers happened to be taller than he.

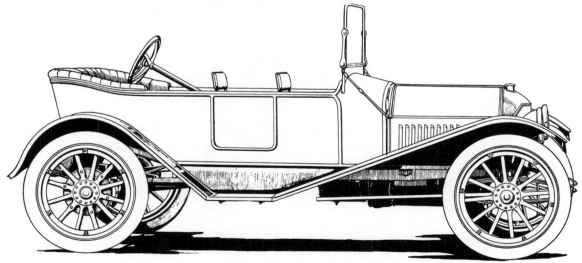

Vulcan, in Greek mythology, was the god of fire, and the Vulcan automobile slogan was one of the most colorful—"Like a Thunderbolt from a Clear Sky." In 1914 Vulcan produced a $750 Roadster (below) which they claimed would turn in a 15-foot radius.

# LIKE A THUNDER BOLT

Also made with 5 passenger Touring Car Body (115″ wheel base) Completely equipped **$850**

**from a clear sky THE**

## VULCAN

### 1914 Announcement

comes as a surprise (but a welcome one) to every dealer.

Vulcan 27 Speedster Completely equipped **$750**

## The World's Greatest Light Car.

**The clean cut Vulcan Chassis—Study the construction.**

### THE VULCAN PLATFORM
27 Horse-power.
3¾″ bore—5″ stroke.
Unit power plant—3 point suspension.
105″ wheel base.
32x3½ tires all round.
3 speed sliding gear transmission.
5 pinion bevel gear differential.
Left side drive.
Center control.
"Streamline" bodies.

Built strong and durable.
Pleasing and graceful lines.
Simple in design and construction.
Easy to operate and steer.
Will turn in 15 feet radius.
Comfortable to ride in.
A smooth running vibrationless motor.
Silent in its action.
Powerful and speedy.
Economical on gas, oil and tires.
Will climb **any** hill.
Economical factory management.
A sane sales policy.
Greatest efficiency throughout the organization.

—consequently—
**Greatest value for the money**

**FITS THE TREMENDOUS DEMAND**
Thousands of dealers and prospective owners have been watching and waiting for the right car at the right price. **You** have often predicted that **some one** would bring out a car that would adequately fill the great popular demand. Others have hit all around the mark, but the Vulcan is the first to hit the bull's-eye.

**A TRULY REMARKABLE CAR**
A machine which takes its place in the front rank immediately—far in advance of anything yet announced. Will climb any hill where the wheels will hold, and stand the severest tests to which a motor can be subjected. Built, not "assembled" only. A car with no objectionable features.

**WE CAN DELIVER THE GOODS**
The Vulcan is being manufactured on an extensive scale. It will be one of the most important factors in the light car field for 1914. In addition to our present large factories, we are preparing to invest millions in additional capacity. Arrangements are already in force, whereby the growth of the plant will keep steady pace with the demands of our dealers.
The Vulcan is not of "Mushroom Growth"—Years have been spent in the perfection of the car and equipping to manufacture in large quantities.
This announcement is not premature, but has been purposely withheld until the progress reached the point when deliveries of 1914 models could be positively assured.

**DEALERS GET IN LINE**
This is your opportunity, but quick action is imperative—we shall not over-sell our capacity—we are appointing only a limited number of the best dealers—no more than we are able to supply with a reasonable number of cars during the season. The Vulcan dealer's agreement is the fairest ever offered. Protects the dealer as well as the producer. Automatic renewal feature makes the dealer a permanent part of the sales organization.
Wire by Night Message for option on your city or town, pending arrival of letter.

**SEND FOR CATALOG**
Send for 1914 Complete Illustrated *Catalog*, describing the product, our facilities and methods.

## Vulcan Mfg Co.

### PAINESVILLE, OHIO, U.S.A.
LOCK BOX PJ 477

# Automobile Slogans of Yesteryear

ALLEN—Wonderful Power, the King of the Hill Climbers.

AMERICAN—Miles of Smiles.

ANDERSON—The Season's Most Enchanting Car.

AUBURN—Once an Owner, Always a Friend.

AUSTIN—A Car to Run Around In.

BEGGS—Made a Little Better Than Seems Necessary.

BUICK—When Better Automobiles Are Built, Buick Will Build Them.

CADILLAC—Standard of the World.

CARTERCAR—No Clutch to Slip, No Gears to Strip.

CHANDLER—The Car of the Year.

COLE—The World's Safest Car.

COLUMBIA—Gem of the Highway.

COMMONWEALTH—The Car with the Foundation.

CONTINENTAL BEACON—The Lowest Priced Full-Sized Car in the World.

DANIELS—The Distinguished Car, with Just a Little More Power Than You'll Ever Need.

DE VAUX—A Jewel for Beauty.

DIANA—The Easiest Steering Car in America.

DODGE—Dependable.

DORRIS—Built Up to a Standard Not Down to a Price.

DRIGGS—Built with the Precision of Ordnance.

DUESENBERG—The World's Champion Automobile.

DUPONT—The Car That Makes an Instant Appeal.

DURANT—Just a Real Good Car.

DURYEA—A Carriage, Not a Machine.

ELGIN—World's Champion Light 6.

ELMORE—The Car That Has No Valves.

EMPIRE—The Little Aristocrat.

FALCON-KNIGHT—America's Finest Type of Motor.

FLINT—The Sensation of the Year.

FORD—The Universal Car.

GAS AU LEC—The Simple Car.

GEARLESS—A Common Sense Car with No Tender or Delicate Parts.

GLIDE—Ride in a Glide, Then Decide.

HANDLEY-KNIGHT—For the Fine Car Owner Who Drives from Choice.

HANOVER—Saves Money Every Mile.

HAYNES-APPERSON—America's First Car.

HUDSON—Look for the White Triangle.
JACKSON—No Hill Too Steep, No Sand Too Deep.
JEWETT—In All the World, No Car Like This (A Bear for Service).
KING—The Car of No Regrets.
KISSEL—The Custom-Built Car.
KLINE—The Ace of the Highway.
LEACH—The Master Creation of the Year.
LIBERTY—All the World Loves a Winner.
LINCOLN—Get Behind the Wheel.
MARMON—Easiest Riding Car in the World.
MARTIN—The Little Brother of the Aeroplane.
MAXWELL—Perfectly Simple—Simply Perfect.
MAYTAG—The Hill Climber.
METZ—The Car You'll Be Proud to Own.
MOORE—The World's Biggest Little Automobile.
NASH—Leads the World in Motor Car Value.
NATIONAL—The All-Ball-Bearing Car.
OLDSMOBILE—Nothing to Watch but the Road.
PACKARD—Ask the Man Who Owns One.
PAIGE—The Most Beautiful Car in America.
PIERCE-ARROW—Pride of Its Makers Makes You Proud in Possession.
PILOT—The Car Ahead.
POPE-TOLEDO—The Quiet, Mile-a-Minute Car.
PREMIER—The Aluminum 6 with Magnetic Gear Shift.
REO—The Gold Standard of Values.
RICKENBACKER—A Car Worthy of Its Name.
ROAMER—America's Smartest Car.
SEARS—The Businessman's Car.
SHERIDAN—The Car Complete.
STANDARD—A Powerful Car.
STAR—Worth the Money.
STEPHENS—'Tis a Great Car.
STEVENS-DURYEA—There Is No Better Motor Car.
STUDEBAKER—The Automobile with a Reputation Behind It.
TEMPLAR—The Superfine Small Car.
VAUGHAN—Made in the Carolinas.
WESTCOTT—The Car with a Longer Life.

# Auto Racing

THIRTY years ago automobile racing contributed more to the industry than it does today. A young industry had to dramatize its product to capture the imagination of the public, and smart promoters thought up the Glidden Tours, the Vanderbilt Cup Race, and the Indianapolis Speedway. There is a direct relationship between these famous auto events of yesterday and America's fine highway system and excellent automobiles of today. Modern automobile racing, however, lacks the spirit that was Barney Oldfield's. The racing pioneers did much to improve and establish the automobile. Today race fans see a different style of racing—midgets on small tracks, stock cars, and Hot Rods. . . . In the chain-driven car below, J. Frank Duryea (behind the tiller) won the first automobile race held in America. He traveled 54 miles from Chicago to Evanston and back at an average speed of 5 miles per hour.

A great deal of valuable engineering data resulted from the exploits of early racing-car drivers like Oldfield, Mulford, DePalma, Cooper, Robertson, and others. Year by year as the speeds increased at the tracks, engineers cut down the size of their engines, and some added superchargers. This principle of lighter but more powerful engines was reflected immediately in the commercial field. Racing achieved great popularity almost immediately. The first race in America was held in 1895, and only fourteen years later the great mecca of the speed fans, with a spectator capacity of over 100,000, was built at Indianapolis. The philosophy of the American auto racer might be likened to that of the Spanish bullfighter. They both seek excitement, tempt fate, and deal with death as part of their daily routine.

One of the earliest racing cars was a Stanley Steamer (below) in which F. E. Stanley covered a mile in 1 minute, 2⅘ seconds in 1903. The next year Henry Ford drove his famous racer, the "999" (bottom left), to victory in a dual race with a Mr. Harkness.

139

## White Races His Own Steamer

The Vanderbilt Cup Race, sanctioned by the American Automobile Association, was held at Mineola, Long Island, until it was discontinued in 1914. The event was so important to automobile companies that sometimes their top officials—like Walter C. White (two photos below) in the 1905 Vanderbilt—drove their own cars. White drove one of his own Steamers.

## Vanderbilt Cup Race of 1908

The Vanderbilt Cup Contest was so popular that eventually it had to be abandoned. The police were unable to restrain the crowds from risking their necks on the highway just to catch a glimpse of the speeding cars. The result was that only a narrow lane remained for the drivers, and spectators and contestants alike were often injured.

In 1908 George Robertson, whose photograph in 1908 and in 1948 is on page 73, broke all Vanderbilt Cup records by racing 258 miles at 64 miles per hour, and on a wet day at that. On this page a photographer (left) and *Esquire* artist Peter Helck (bottom) have a try at immortalizing the same scene—and what a triumph it is for vital art over static reality!

### The 90 H. P. *Locomobile*

Driven by George Robertson, winning the Vanderbilt Cup Race, the Greatest International Automobile Competition and the Supreme Test of Reliability and Endurance.   In Spite of the Slippery Course the 258 Miles were Covered at an Average Rate of Speed of 64.3 Miles an Hour, Breaking all Records Established in Previous Contests for this Famous Trophy.

141

## New York to Paris, 1908

Fifty thousand curious and doubting persons were on hand at Times Square in New York City on the morning of February 12, 1908, to witness the start of the strangest and longest automobile race in history. Two newspapers, *The New York Times* and *Le Matin* of Paris, were sponsoring a round-the-world race, and there were six entrants: three French, one German, one Italian, and one American. The route took them overland to San Francisco; by boat to Valdez, Alaska; across Alaska to Fairbanks and then to Nome; across the Bering Strait (on ice) to Vladivostok; across Siberia to Russia; and across Germany, Belgium, and France to Paris. Three cars completed the 13,431-mile race and the winner—the famous Thomas Flyer driven by two Americans, Montague Roberts and George Schuster—arrived in Paris on July 30, 170 days after leaving Times Square. The two top photos were taken in Times Square, February 12. The American car followed the railroad track through heavy Indiana snow (third photo). Below, the Thomas Flyer, damaged by fire, is now being restored to original condition.

J. Frank Duryea won the first American automobile race between Chicago and Evanston, Illinois, in 1895. Fifty years later, in 1945, the Chicago Museum of Science and Industry sponsored a reenactment of that initial contest and offered an unusual display of old cars in the museum. At right is an engraved announcement of the Golden Jubilee Celebration and below two full-dress street scenes of early Chicago (Museum of Science and Industry exhibit). A Haynes-Apperson is parked at the curb on the left (top photo) and a high-wheeled International Auto Buggy is parked in front of the Hub. The car in the lower photo is a Baker Electric, and the Nickelodeon in the background was the forefather of our modern movie.

*The Museum of Science and Industry Chicago announces with pleasure A Golden Jubilee Celebration of the First Automobile Race in America held in November 1895 with the Museum as the starting point Special Commemorative Exhibits of fifty years of automotive progress will be opened on November 2, 1945 Appropriate events will be held during the month culminating in a run by early cars over the original course on Thanksgiving Day*

143

## The Three P's, 1913

Iᴛ was often said in the years before World War I that "the three P's" were the cars of quality —the Packard, the Peerless, and the Pierce-Arrow. For those who did not have to keep a tight hold on their purse strings, the 1913 Pierce-Arrow (below), with its sleek and shiny exterior and plush interior, was just the right buy. Of course the car called for a chauffeur—and the chauffeur called for a severely tailored uniform.

Interior 38 Horse-power, Model C, Six-cylinder Pierce-Arrow Brougham

38 Horse-power, Six-cylinder Pierce-Arrow Brougham, Model C, seating five persons

144

When the price is an asset, the automobile advertisement states the price in heavy print. When the price is high, the advertisement forgets to mention it and inserts a saluting chauffeur instead. The 1914 International Cycle Car (top) sold at the amazingly low figure of $380, and the Metz (lower left) cost $475. The Columbus Electric (lower right) makes no mention of price but it does employ a liveried chauffeur and such expressions as "evident richness, air of distinction, and exclusiveness." The Metz "22" had a gearless transmission which made it "a good car for grocers . . . collecting orders and making light deliveries."

**Price $380, f. o. b., Harvey, Ill.**
Shield and Top, $15 Extra

# Winner of the Glidden Tour

Quality wins. Competing with many of America's expensive and best-known cars, over an extremely difficult course embracing all conditions of endurance-testing roads and hills, the METZ team of three regular stock cars was the ONLY team that held a perfect score for the entire eight days of the contest.

**A Good Car for Grocers.** Saves time in collecting orders and making light deliveries.

**A Practical car for Town or Country**

1914 IMPROVEMENTS EQUIPPED COMPLETE

## METZ "22"—$475

### The Gearless Car

*"No clutch to slip —— No gears to strip"*

A remarkable example of low price and minimum cost of upkeep combined with the essenial features of the up-to-date car—a car that affords luxury without extravagance.

The METZ "22" is a high class, fully guaranteed roadster of the torpedo semi-enclosed type, left-hand drive and center control. Under ordinary road conditions it travels 28 to 32 miles on one gallon of gasoline, 100 miles on a pint of lubricating oil, and 10,000 to 12,000 miles on a single set of tires.

Equipped with 4-cylinder 22½ H. P. water-cooled motor, *Bosch magneto*, wind shield, extension top and cover slip, full elliptic springs all around, standard artillery wheels, best quality *Goodrich clincher tires*, 5 lamps and gas generator, horn, pump and tool outfit. Its gearless

transmission entirely does away with gear troubles.

Will make from 5 to 50 miles per hour on the high speed, and climbs hills as fast as any regular stock car made. Built to carry either single or double rumble seat, if desired.

**Write for our New Illustrated Catalog "H"**

When equipped with best electric starter, electric head lights, electric side lights, electric dash and tail lights and electric horn, price is $600.00.

**We want a representative in every city and town. Write for terms.**

**METZ COMPANY, WALTHAM, MASS.**

THE COLUMBVS ELECTRIC

## The Town Car for All the Family

¶ Just glance a moment at the above illustration of our 1912 Model 1225 and imagine it standing in front of your home! Does it not appeal to you instantly by its artistic design; its evident richness of finish, its air of distinction and exclusiveness? Add to this, ease of operation, comfort, safety, ample speed and low cost of maintenance; the absence of oil, smoke, dirt and noise, and you have all that you can possibly obtain in any motor vehicle.

¶ The COLUMBUS-ELECTRIC will give all the service a man can ask, yet it is so simply constructed, so easily controlled, that a woman or even a child can run it safely. There is no complicated machinery to worry about, just a lever to push—that's all. No matter how bad the weather, you can go anywhere you like in town in cozy comfort, as fast as any city ordinance will permit, and at not much more cost than street car fare.

*Write for Catalog 64-E.*

### THE COLUMBUS BUGGY COMPANY

564 Dublin Avenue,                    Columbus, Ohio

## Car Tows Airplane, 1913

In 1913, a year for new ideas, the Wahl Motor Company in Detroit advertised cars without trade-marks so that dealers could put their own names and trade-marks on the radiator. Glenn L. Martin, maker of famous airplanes, announced the creation of the first "family airplane." M. Sterling Burgess, another early aviator and designer, towed his airplane from the factory through the streets of Boston to an aviation field, using his White "30" (below). The 1914 Studebaker Touring Car (bottom photo) had hickory wheels with demountable rims.

In the year 1914 the Archduke Francis Ferdinand, heir to the Austrian Empire, was assassinated with his wife in the streets of Sarajevo in Bosnia. Most Americans considered the murder only another incident in the turbulent politics of the Balkans and went right back to reading the Ford ad (below) promising that buyers of the $750 Coupelet "will share in profits if we sell at retail 300,000 new Fords between August, 1914, and August, 1915." It was once Ford's self-avowed ambition to produce a light, strong car "that was clean enough for women to drive." The 1914 ad for this stylish convertible claimed that it was "especially popular with women . . . convenient and exclusive as an electric."

## Ford Coupelet $750
**(Fully Equipped, f. o. b. Detroit)**

This car is the most practical two-passenger model we have ever built. When the top is folded, the Coupelet becomes an open Runabout of unusual smartness and style.

The change from closed to open car can be made in two minutes, so that the Coupelet is quickly adaptable to all conditions of weather and driving.

It is especially popular with women who drive their own cars. As convenient and exclusive as an electric.

For physicians, architects, contractors, and all business and professional men who have to cover a great deal of territory it is admirably suited.

The Ford Coupelet may be driven twelve months in the year, in the city or over country roads, without personal discomfort, no matter what the weather.

Its distinctive style and attractiveness give it an exclusive appearance not found in any open runabout.

Buyers of this car will share in profits if we sell at retail 300,000 new Ford cars between August, 1914, and August, 1915.

## Streamline in 1914

The body of this 1914 Maxwell would look square as a box to modern car connoisseurs but the ads of the day called it the "pure streamline body." The "gracefully rounded double-shell radiator" had a very functional shock absorber inside to protect the radiator from vibration. This was the cheapest 4-cylinder car Maxwell ever produced, $695.

The electrically operated push-button doors on this 1914 Scripps-Booth were way ahead of their time. The Scripps-Booth is one of hundreds of now extinct cars once made in Detroit. The list would include such forgotten makes as the Demot, Abbott-Detroit, Chalmers, Ross, Harroun, Flanders, Read, Monarch, Jewett, E.M.F., Northern, and many others.

# SCRIPPS BOOTH

## Luxurious Light Cars

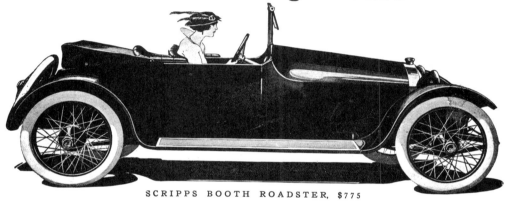

SCRIPPS BOOTH ROADSTER, $775

## SPECIFICATIONS:

*110-inch wheelbase, three passenger car.*

### MECHANISM

*Four-cylinder motor, three-speed gearset, shaft drive, bevel gear rear axle.*

### EQUIPMENT

*Absolutely complete from electric self-starting and lighting system to electric door locks.*

### FINISH

*Finest possible, both as regards upholstery, instruments, dash equipment and body finish.*

### DETAILS

*Body—Streamline, torpedo stern, highest grade blue-black finish, domed fenders. Upholstery, finest quality long-grain buffed leather. Cowl dash instruments; sight feed oiler, lighting and dimming switches, starting strangler, starting and ignition switch, flush type speedometer, generator indicator, shroud light and foot space light.*

### WHEELS

*Five Houk, triple-laced detachable wire, 30x3½ inches, wide hubs.*

### AXLE

*Rear, full-floating, annular bearings throughout. Bevel drive. Ball bearing universal joints on the Kardan shaft. All gears and shafts 3½% nickel steel. Drive shaft tubular.*

### W O R T H

in a motor car is not figured by pounds weight, gross dimensions, or dollar-cost units.

### E X P E N S E

in running a car is not figured in money alone.

### EXTREME VALUE

combines the maximum worth of luxury with a minimum of discomforts; the extreme of **comfort-efficiency** engineering with the minimum of motoring troubles.

### The Basis of Comfort Value

is light weight with highest grade construction, best expressed in SCRIPPS BOOTH luxurious light cars, as shown by the following specification outline:

## SCRIPPS-BOOTH CO.
### DETROIT

## SPECIFICATIONS:

### MOTOR

*Sterling, valve-in-head type, high speed, gearset in unit, pump feed oiling with sight feed on dash, 2⅞ bore, 4-inch stroke, four-cylinder, water cooled. Develops 18 horsepower. Fitted with Zenith carbureter and Atwater-Kent automatic spark advance, connected with starter generator system.*

### STARTING

*Bijur single unit electric, connected by silent chain, operated by locking dash switch.*

### SPRINGS

*Front, semi-elliptic with over-slung frame. Rear, floating cantilever.*

### EQUIPMENT

*Silk mohair top with side curtains, rain vision plate glass windshield, electric door lock, Klaxet horn, full tool equipment, jack. Luggage space at the rear large enough for two suit-cases and tools. Spare Houk wheel, tire and tube on all cars.*

### FEATURES

*Klaxet button in center of steering wheel cannot be operated when ignition switch is off, eliminating miscellaneous horn blowing while the car is standing.*

*No projecting handles or slots in the doors. Electric door locks are operated by pressing a small push button.*

149

## *Studebaker Catalogue, 1915*

Below is a reproduction of a page from the 1915 Studebaker catalogue. Both of these long sleek models had six-cylinder engines and were leather-upholstered. The four-passenger coupé at top sold for $1,550 and the seven-passenger touring car for $1,050.

### SIX-Fifty Four Passenger Coupe

This view shows the beautiful design and lines of the new SIX-Fifty Four Passenger Coupe. The driver's seating arrangement is similar to that of the Roadster. There is an auxiliary seat, however, forward at the right. This seat folds forward under the cowl, the legs disappearing into the floor similar to that of the 1915 touring car auxiliary seat. These coupes are upholstered in genuine hand-buffed straight grain enamel-finish leather or in any of the three styles of Bedford cord. The interior finish is as luxurious and beautiful as it is possible to make a closed car. The tire carrying compartment at the rear is the same as that of the Roadster.

### Studebaker Six-Seven Passenger Touring Car

Auxiliary seats disappearing into the floor; straight grain, genuine buffed leather, semi-gloss surface; divided front seat; robe and foot rail; 34 x 4 tires; new easy acting one man top. This car is easily one of the most powerful six-cylinder seven-passenger cars on the market. Its beautiful finish, roominess, richness of upholstery, depth of cushions, seat sides and backs stamp it unmistakably as a wonderful car at any price. Its great power, flexibility, ease of control, smoothness of operation show its splendid mechanical qualities. This six-cylinder can be demonstrated with any car at any price, six, eight or even twelve cylinders and its action will charm even the most particular prospect.

The Partin-Palmer "20" offered a steering-wheel shaft as long as a giraffe's neck, a "full-floating rear axle," three speeds forward, a speedometer, and wooden wheels—all for the low price of $495. In 1914 advertising experts did not put much faith in subtlety.

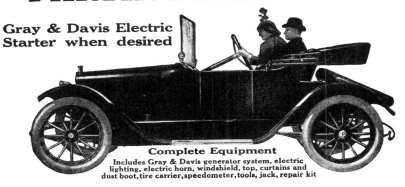

## The Air-cooled Franklin, 1915

The expensive cars had gentler ads. This $2,150 air-cooled Franklin had a front-sloping hood that opened from the front. Franklin cars featured a wooden frame, wooden front axle, and full elliptic springs, front and rear, which gave a surprisingly easy ride.

# FRANKLIN

### *You Use it all the Time—*
### *50 degrees below Zero, 120 degrees in the Shade*

IN Strassburg, in the 12th Century, there was built a wonderful clock. It rang all sorts of bells. It gave the phases of the Moon. It was full of wheels and pipes and pulleys. It was so wonderfully complicated it required constant attention. So they only ran it on Sundays and Fete days, and on these days it told the time.

Then some bold spirits said—Give us a clock that will run all the time!

That is about what has happened with the automobile.

Men used to brag about what they had in their car. Now they tell you what they have gotten rid of. They are looking for *simplicity*, not complexity.

They used to think that with a multiplicity of parts they were getting more for their money—radiator, pipes, fittings, gears in the fly-wheel, automatic devices in connection with the starter, spark control, torque, reach and other kinds of rods tying the axle to a ponderous body.

Now they know that every time they get rid of something on an automobile they add to their peace of mind.

The Franklin achieved one of the biggest things in the automobile business when it established direct-air-cooling and *did away with plumbing.* Nothing to freeze in winter or boil in summer. No radiator to nurse up the hill on a hot day or to blanket every time you draw up to the curb in cold weather. No fussing with anti-freezing mixtures.

A car that you can use all the time.

59 per cent. of Franklin owners are men who have owned other standard makes of automobiles.

There are so many things about the Franklin that are different. There are so many results obtained in its use that are different, in comfort, luxury and easy riding qualities, that these men never get over telling you how it does everything any other car ever did for them—does it better and at less cost of operation.

Every one is aware now of the growing interest in air-cooling both in this country and in Europe.

The Franklin over a period of fourteen years has perfected a direct-air-cooling system that is attracting the attention of the world.

If you want to know how satisfactory is the Franklin direct-air-cooling system, talk to a Franklin owner, or go to a Franklin dealer and ask him to show you how thoroughly Franklin direct-air-cooling *cools.*

The Franklin National Cooling Test settled that question for all time, when on September 24, 1914, 116 Franklin stock cars in 116 parts of the country ran 100 miles each on low gear without stopping the engine.

Among fine cars the Franklin is the exponent of scientific light-weight.

The Franklin Six - Thirty Touring Car weighs 2750 pounds and the price is $2150.

### FRANKLIN AUTOMOBILE COMPANY
#### SYRACUSE, N. Y.

152

# Wisconsin, Erstwhile Auto Capital

WHEN a young industry is in the invention instead of the production stage, factors like raw material or transportation facilities or labor supply are for the most part irrelevant. The inventor works in his back yard or in a barn or in a small garage, and his project calls for a solo effort. By 1914, however, there were 1,258,000 registered automobiles in the United States, and Henry Ford alone was striving to produce 300,000 cars a year. It was inevitable that the whole automobile industry should gravitate in some direction and find a center. Cincinnati, because of the many types of carriages manufactured there, was an applicant, and Cleveland was an up-and-coming town which offered access to the Great Lakes. Indianapolis, Milwaukee, and Detroit were the other main candidates.

Though Detroit and its satellite neighbors are today the home of the automobile industry, Wisconsin and Milwaukee had much to offer the business. Many pioneers of Wisconsin will tell you that more than eighty different makes of cars and trucks have been manufactured in Wisconsin since 1900, although now there are only two corporations making pleasure cars and four making trucks exclusively in the state. Wisconsinites will tell you that the first successful steam car driven on any highway in the United States was made in 1872 in Racine by Dr. J. W. Carhart, and that the first practical gasoline-powered car in the nation was built in Milwaukee in 1889 by Gottfried Schloemer, a mechanically inclined barrel-maker.

They also claim that Duryea or Winton did not sell the first automobile in the United States but that A. W. Ballard, an Oshkosh bicycle repairman, made a car to order for a physician living in Wausau, Wisconsin, in 1895. They contend, too, that the first automobile race in the world was in 1878 between two steam wagons that raced from Green Bay to Madison. One of the steam cars is said to have completed the distance at an average speed of 6 miles per hour. This race was an effort to win a $10,000 prize put up by the legislature for the first practical self-propelled highway vehicle.

More than four million automotive vehicles have been made in Wisconsin. The two biggest Wisconsin companies, Chevrolet (assembly plant) and Nash, still operate there. Ancestors of the Nash were the Rambler and Jeffery, early Wisconsin makes. Other famous cars once made in Wisconsin include the Case and the Mitchell of Racine; the Kissel Kar of Hartford; and the Lafayette of both Milwaukee and Kenosha. Less-known Wisconsin makes were the Hayberg, an air-cooled car that sold for $2,000; the Monarch; the Pennington; the Merkel, built by Joe Merkel, who later built the Merkel Motorcycle; the Superior, a single experimental car manufactured in Milwaukee by S. E. Briggs and H. M. Stratton from manufacturers' units; the Kunz; the Pierce-Racine; the Earl; the F.W.D. Battship at Clintonville, using a four-wheel-drive principle; the Petrel friction-drive car; the Ogren, made in Milwaukee from 1919 to 1922; the Badger "30"; the Vixen Cyclecar; the Johnson Steamer; and many others.

153

*A Saxon, $395*

No matter what the model, no matter what the value of your dollar, $395 is not much to spend for an automobile. The now scarcely remembered Saxon was once a household word.

*New improved body, genuine streamline effect— identical in style with high priced two-passenger cars. Wood or wire wheels. Electric lights and starter, $70. Standard or 60-inch tread.*

154

In 1915, 895,930 cars were manufactured, about 890,000 more than were produced in 1900. Austin (below) offered a unique two-speed rear axle and rear cantilever springs.

# AUSTIN

| TWO SPEED AXLE | SIX CYLINDER 4½ X 6 | DOUBLE CANTILEVER SPRINGS |

AUSTIN CLOSE-COUPLED TOURING CAR has ample room for three passengers on both the front and rear seats.

THE AUSTIN TWO-SPEED AXLE combines all the advantages of a special high gear and a normal or regular gear, and we want you to appreciate and realize that the AUSTIN special direct drive on the 2 to 1 gear ratio, has the same proportional advantages and superiority in smoothness, quietness, durability and economy over the normal or regular drive, that the normal or regular direct drive has over the second speed, through the transmission gears, in the common car construction.

**All claims of superior merit must be based upon a material difference in design which will show indisputable mechanical reasons why such distinctive design will give better results.**

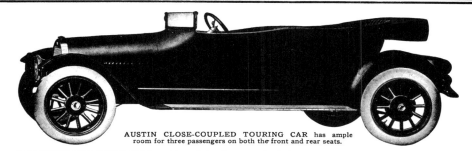

AUSTIN TOURING ROADSTER, when furnished with an undivided seat, has ample room for three people.

AUSTIN DOUBLE CANTILEVER SPRINGS support the car weight by two light springs on each side, instead of one stiff spring, giving a much softer and easier riding car.

These light, flexible springs with a divided load are not nearly as apt to become broken as any stiffer spring would be that has to carry the full load. The rear weight on each side is distributed to four different points, and if one of these springs should be broken at one end, there would still remain three-quarters of our spring capacity on that side which would be ample to finish any drive.

Please note the advantages of this close-coupled body where all the passengers are placed forward of the rear axle in the most desirable location for easy riding, and also securing practically an even distribution of weight on both axles. This is also a great factor of safety, as the danger of skidding is practically eliminated.

**Write for further information regarding our distinctive and exclusive features**

# AUSTIN AUTOMOBILE COMPANY

## GRAND RAPIDS, MICHIGAN

# Automobile Advertising

ADVERTISEMENTS today are slick and tricky. Fifty years ago they were full-voiced and red-blooded. In 1903 one long-forgotten Dr. H. Nelson Jackson drove a Winton touring car across the continent, and the Winton Motor Carriage Company made advertising capital of the stunt. According to the announcement below, "malicious stories" were circulated (by envious competitors, of course) that the mysterious Dr. Jackson had never made the trip and that the whole thing was a fraud. Roaring like two wounded lions, the Winton Company and the doctor reared back on their hind legs and offered $25,000 reward to anyone who could supply any evidence substantiating "this anvil chorus of malicious stories."

# $25,000 REWARD!!!

LAST week we offered $10,000.00 to anyone who could produce the slightest evidence showing the truth in any of the various malicious stories told by the "anvil chorus" about Dr. H. Nelson Jackson and his successful transcontinental ride with a Winton Touring Car. To date no one has appeared to claim the reward. The attacks upon Dr. Jackson's honor have pleased him no more than they have us, and he has authorized us to add $15,000 to our original reward, so we raise the amount and now offer

## TWENTY-FIVE THOUSAND DOLLARS

This amount we will pay to anyone proving that at any time on his journey across the Continent conditions of transportation were other than represented by Dr. Jackson.

Dr. Jackson's great triumph with his regular model Winton is a bit discomfiting to some others interested in transcontinental "stunts," especially when it is considered that he is not a mechanic, nor was he accompanied by a factory mechanic, or met at frequent intervals *en route* by factory mechanics with parts and supplies of all kinds. But the fact remains that aside from showing himself a clever amateur sportsman and a good automobilist, he demonstrated beyond question that the Winton Touring Car is the best automobile for long-distance touring manufactured or sold in America.

**Send for Booklet illustrating and describing the first successful Ocean-to-Ocean automobile ride**

## THE WINTON MOTOR CARRIAGE CO.

FACTORY AND HEAD OFFICE:

### CLEVELAND, Ohio, U. S. A.

The format of this 1905 Cadillac ad is the dignified design that we have learned to expect. On closer inspection, however, the ad has its rough spots. In the second line of small print, it states that "he (the competitor) don't know what he's talking about." Cadillac admen have picked up a lot of grammar since 1905. The photograph is a rear view of a man driving a Cadillac up the steps of the Capitol building in Washington. The implication is that it's all in the pursuit of technical knowledge: the young engineer testing his car's pulling power. However, historical sources have recently revealed that an enterprising Cadillac adman filled the youth with hard cider, convinced him it was part of a fraternity initiation, bound him hand and foot to the steering lever, and turned the crank himself. Cadillac's cryptic and ambiguous remark (beneath the photo) is "He paid for his fun. . . ."

# When a Competitor Tells You

that we are going to remodel our motor and increase the cylinder capacity in order to get greater power, he don't know what he's talking about. We're going to do nothing of the kind. We don't need to. We had more power in that little 5 x 5 engine of last year than was needed for ordinary work. It was tried at extraordinary work and was not found lacking. Think what it means to hook onto a load of street railway iron (seven seventy foot rails) loaded on two trucks, requiring four heavy horses to pull, the estimated weight of steel and trucks being over eight tons, and draw that load up a four per cent. grade from a standing start. A Canton (Ohio) Cadillac owner (Mr. A. H. Wilson) did it, not only once but several times. A two-cylinder opposed engine, rated at 8 horsepower, tried it and failed to move it forward an inch. Remodel the Cadillac Engine? Certainly not; there's no reason for it. When anyone tells you this

# Don't You Believe Him

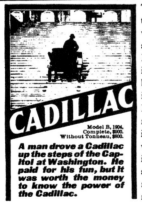

**Model B, 1904.**
Complete, $900.
Without Tonneau, $800.

*A man drove a Cadillac up the steps of the Capitol at Washington. He paid for his fun, but it was worth the money to know the power of the Cadillac.*

The Cadillac Engine of last year had ample power (it's got more this year) for those who *knew* how to operate it. A large cylinder would be no advantage to those who *do not* know how to secure all the available power a gas engine is capable of. The Cadillac Motor is, and always has been a wonder. Competitors recognized it from the first minute after it came out. Some of them have been busy "knocking" ever since; others "got wise" and made imitations; others "sawed wood;" but all are guessing. When Leland & Faulconer Manufacturing Co. makes anything, it is as near right as fine tools, gauges, dies, machinery and men assembled in a well organized and old established firm can make it. And when they tell you it has a certain horsepower, you can bank on its having more. This well known firm makes all Cadillac Motors and transmissions, and they are made well. Speaking of Transmissions reminds us—but never mind, we'll tell you about those next week; we are "all in" for want of space.

## CADILLAC AUTOMOBILE COMPANY

*Members of the Association of Licensed Automobile Manufacturers*

**DETROIT, MICH.**

**ALL EYES ON THE ELMORE**

All we've got to say to you is this:—Don't spend $2500 for a four-cylinder, four-cycle automobile till you've seen the 16 H. P., double-cylinder, 2-cycle Elmore at $1250. Don't do it, because there are regrets ahead of you if you do. And this is why

**The ELMORE at $1250**

produces precisely the same power with its double-cylinder, two-cycle engine as a 4-cylinder, 4-cycle car of the same size and speed—with 75 per cent less parts. Using the throttle and without manipulating any clutches it can be immediately controlled from two to thirty miles an hour. Uphill or straight away, on any road, it can be handled on the high-speed more effectively than any car in America. The two-cycle engine produces TWO impulses with every revolution of the fly-wheel, furnishing a continuous application of power absolutely without waste.

We say again—before you consider a car at $2500 or any other price you owe it to yourself to read all you can about the Elmore and see it in operation.

*Send for the 1905 catalogue, "The Cruise of the Pathfinder," describing its celebrated runs from New York to St. Louis and return, and the interesting book describing the principle of the two-cycle engine.*

10 x 12 mounted photographs of the $1250.00 side entrance Elmore, 10c. in stamps.

**THE ELMORE MFG. CO., 504 Amanda St., Clyde, Ohio**
Member of the Association of Licensed Automobile Mfrs.

These ads were considered distinctive and effective in their time. Each used a different device. The motorists at the top of the Elmore ad (left) looked so pleased by the object of their attention that the reader must automatically follow their glance and in turn admire the $1,250 Elmore. "The Beau Brummel of the Road" ad (bottom, left) flatters our vanity and implies that all we need to be the "spit and image" of that monocled fashion plate is a Yale automobile in which to "dash down the road, a flash of gold and blue." The Gas-au-lec (below, right) adopts the straightforward take-it-or-leave-it approach. Theirs is "The Simple Car." That's all. They're not going to twist your arm.

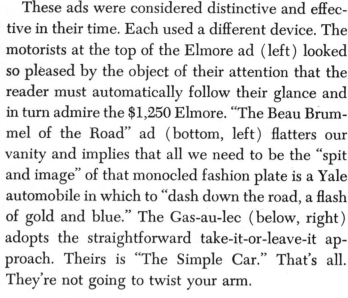

**GAS·AU·LEC**
**"THE SIMPLE CAR"**

**THE BEAU BRUMMEL OF THE ROAD**

2 CYLINDER 14 H.P. **The Yale** $2500.00

$1000.00

Try to picture to yourself the prettiest Touraround that ever dashed down a country road—a flash of gold and blue, whizzing by with no more noise than a mere musical whirring of wheels. Then try to conceive a car so filled with power that it is like a living thing; and so instantaneously responsive that it can be controlled by a touch of the thumb and index finger. When you've formed this mental impression—you've just begun to get an unexaggerated notion of the thousand dollar

**Yale for 1905!**
Side Entrance $1100.

The new double-cylinder Yale weighs only 1400 pounds—with a full ounce of continuous power for every ounce of weight, and some to spare.

You mustn't even think of finally considering any other car at anywhere near the price before you've read, heard and seen more of "the Beau Brummel of the Road"—the thousand dollar Yale for 1905. For the prince of 4-cylinder Touring Cars write us about the superb new 24 H. P. Yale—a triumph of mechanical perfection and completeness.

*New catalogue ready to mail January 1st. Write for it.*

**THE KIRK MFG. CO., 958 Oakwood Ave., Toledo, Ohio**
Member of the Association of Licensed Automobile Manufacturers.

A 40-45 H. P., 4-cylinder, 4-cycle engine, five passenger, side entrance Gasolene Touring Car of the Highest Grade.

**WITHOUT** { Starting Crank; Cams; Valve Gearing
Change Speed Gears; Rocker Shafts; or
Clutch; Tappets; Complications.

Every movement of the motive power and the car, from a state of absolute rest, forward at any speed or reverse, is controlled by one lever, operated either by hand or foot, as preferred. Positively no other speed or movement controlling device of any kind on the car. Triple brakes—irreversible steering gear.

**The Gas-au-lec is the Simplest Gasolene Car in the World,** both as to construction and control, and the easiest to operate and maintain.

**Elegant in Finish.          Luxurious in Appointments.
Built by Skilled Workmen from the Best Materials Obtainable.**

**CORWIN MFG. CO.** Formerly VAUGHN MACHINE CO.
PEABODY, MASS., U. S. A.

**"Marks a New Era in Automobile Construction."**

158

In 1906 this raucous, red-blooded Buick ad did not hesitate to announce its racing victories to the world and even listed the makes it defeated in various competitions. It is not difficult to understand why these competitions loomed larger and larger.

## HATS OFF TO THE BUICK AT ALGONQUIN

### CARS DEFEATED BY THIS CAR

**MODEL G**

Two
Cylinders
22 H.P
$1000

In Class A. Cars costing $1000 and under
Autocar    2 Maxwells    Mitchell
Cadillac    Ford    2 Holsmans

### CARS DEFEATED BY THIS CAR

MODEL F
Two Cylinders, 22 H. P.
$1,250

Full Lamp
Equipment
and six volt
Storage
Batteries—
both cars

In Class B. Cars costing from $1000 to $1750
Stoddard-Dayton    Mitchell    Reo    Rambler

**45 Minutes from Broadway**
(Plus 24 Days and 8 Hours)

On September 9, 1906, at 6:45 p.m. the BUICK transcontinental two-cylinder model "F" touring car reached San Francisco in its recordbreaking trip from New York City, reducing all records by nine days and creating for the first time in the history of automobiles a touring car record between these points.

Let us mail you our catalogue and literature

## Buick Motor Company

FACTORIES: JACKSON AND FLINT, MICHIGAN

CHICAGO BRANCH, 1412-1414 Michigan Avenue
W. J. MEAD, Manager

159

## The Limited-market Approach

Two tycoons, sitting at a window of a plush and exclusive club, comment favorably on a seven-passenger 1912 Stoddard-Dayton, a car obviously not trying for the mass market.

"That's the next car I buy"

The distinctive design of Stoddard-Dayton cars—combined with their reputation for extraordinary service rendered to owners under all conditions of road and weather—has provoked this comment by many a man seeking the perfect car.  All

# Stoddard=Dayton

cars—whether the six-cylinder Stoddard-Dayton Knight, the Special, the Saybrook, or the Savoy—are marked by this distinctive quality, recognizable anywhere.  This is true of them internally as well as externally.

**UNITED STATES MOTOR COMPANY, 17 West 61st Street, New York City**
*(Stoddard-Dayton Division)*

For $7,450 you could buy all this distinction and exclusiveness in 1922. Charles the chauffeur holds the Russian wolfhound while Madame shops. . . . Beautiful ad, small market.

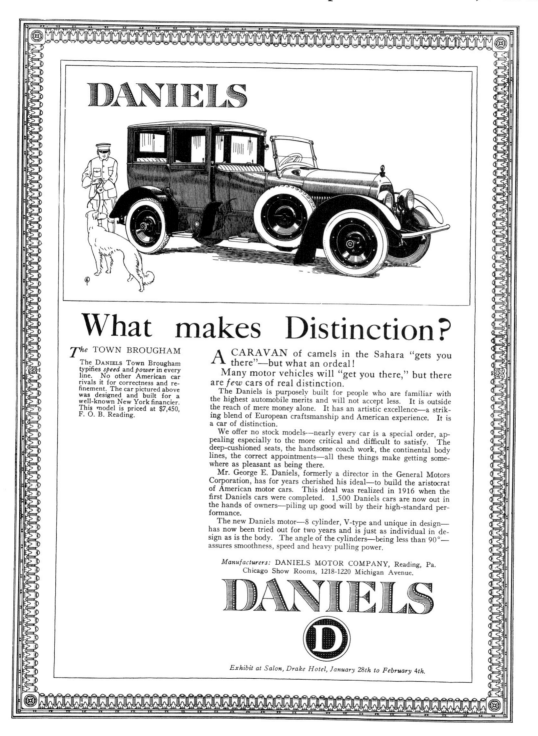

161

# Ransom's Best

Experts consider the following four ads to be among the finest that the industry has produced. Below, designer Ransom E. Olds states flatly that the 1912 Reo is the best he can do.

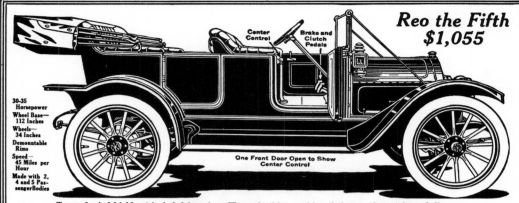

**Reo the Fifth
$1,055**

30-35 Horsepower
Wheel Base—112 Inches
Wheels—34 Inches
Demountable Rims
Speed—45 Miles per Hour
Made with 2, 4 and 5 Passenger Bodies

Center Control

Brake and Clutch Pedals

One Front Door Open to Show Center Control

Top and windshield not included in price. We equip this car with mohair top, side curtains and slip-cover, windshield, gas tank and speedometer—all for $100 extra. SELF-STARTER, IF WANTED, $25 EXTRA

# The Car That Marks My Limit

### By R. E. Olds, Designer

**I have no quarrel with men who ask more for their cars—none with men who ask less. I have only to say that, after 25 years —after creating 24 models and building tens of thousands of cars—here's the best I know. I call it My Farewell Car.**

I claim for this car no great innovation. The time is past for that.

Thousands of good men, for two decades, have worked at perfecting cars. No man can ever go much further than the best these men have done.

I believe that Reo the Fifth, in every feature, shows the utmost these men have accomplished. It represents, in addition, the best I have learned through 25 years of continuous striving. So it comes, I believe, pretty close to finality.

It shows what can be done by modern facilities, by boundless experience, by honesty of purpose, by the genius for taking pains. And that is all that any car at any price can offer.

### The Lessons of 25 Years

Where this car excels lies in what I have learned in 25 years of car building.

I've been learning longer than others. I have learned faster than others, because I had more cars out.

That's my chief advantage.

What some think right, I know to be wrong. What some think sufficient, I know to be reckless.

Myriads of cars used by myriads of owners have taught me every possible weakness. They have shown the need for big margins of safety, for exactness, for careful inspection, for laboratory tests.

### I Go to Extremes

For every part I know the best steel alloy. To make sure that I get it, **I analyze all my steel.**

I built a crushing machine of 50 tons' capacity just to test my gears.

My axles have twice the needed strength. My bearings are Timken Roller and Hyatt High Duty.

My carburetor is **doubly** heated, and adapted to low-grade gasoline. That makes the commonest troubles impossible.

I carry tests and inspections, throughout the construction, to what men call extremes. Those 25 years taught me the need for precautions.

They also have taught me that men love beautiful cars. My bodies are finished with 17 coats. My lamps are enameled—my engine nickel trimmed.

The upholstering is deep, and of hair-filled genuine leather.

The wheel base is long, the wheels are large, the car is over-tired. I avoid all the petty economies.

### New Center Control

The gear shifting is done by that center "cane-handle." It moves only three inches in each of four directions to change to every speed and reverse.

There are no side levers. Both of the brakes, also the clutch, are operated by the foot pedals. The doors are free from obstructions.

The driver may sit — as he should sit—on the left hand side, close to the cars which he passes. With the old lever controls this was impossible, save in electric cars.

### Price, $1,055 the Only Sensation

My greatest achievement, in my estimation, is the price on this new car. No other car begins to compete with it.

This is due to automatic machinery—to enormous production —to making all parts in one factory. It is due to building only one chassis in all this great plant. It is due to small selling cost, and to a very small profit.

But this price is not fixed. This

initial price of $1,055 is the minimum. It is based on today's low cost for materials. It is figured on a doubled output, due to this new creation.

If costs advance our price must advance. But we shall keep it this low just as long as is possible. That is better, we think, than fixing the price for six months in advance, and leaving big margin to do it.

### My Supreme Effort

Reo the Fifth marks my limit. Better materials are impossible, better workmanship out of the question. Better features or devices, if they exist, are still unknown to me.

More care or skill or quality is beyond my capability. At twice the price I could build no better car. If others can, they are better men than I.

### Ask for Catalog

Ask for our catalog, showing the various bodies and stating all the facts. We will tell you then where to see the car.

Reo the Fifth, my finest creation, will interest every motor car lover. Ask for the book today. Address

## R. M. Owen & Co. General Sales Agents for Reo Motor Car Co., Lansing, Mich.

Canadian Factory, St. Catharines, Ontario

In 1918 Ned Jordan started a new era in car advertising with unusual yet subdued phrases like "the first completely equipped motorcar" and sleek, sophisticated tableaux.

## The First Completely Equipped Motor Car

The Jordan Sport Marine is the first completely equipped motor car ever offered as a stock model by a manufacturer. It is a custom made car at a stock car price.

The new Continental motor, introduced by Jordan, eliminates vibration, accentuates speed, increases power and affords a degree of economy and smoothness that is far in advance of the times. The aluminum body is fifty pounds lighter, free from rumbles and ripples and takes that beautiful velvety finish.

Two optional colors, Briarcliff green and Liberty blue. Upholstered in special hand buffed, genuine leather, with velvet tonneau rug. Rim wind sport clock, and tonneau light empanelled in Honduras mahogany.

Because of its completeness, its ultra comfort, its smartness, the Sport Marine is essentially a woman's car.

It is fashionably low with five 32 x 4 wire wheels and five Silvertown Cord Tires, special speed gear ratio, sport windshield, tailored top, traffic bumper, motometer, Macbeth green visor lenses and Lin-Rhubber on running boards as standard equipment. Curtains that open with the doors.

**JORDAN MOTOR CAR COMPANY, CLEVELAND, OHIO**

163

## Cadillac—Real Class

Cadillac's splendid "Penalty of Leadership" advertisement in 1915 set an all-time high for calm, quiet, confident advertisements that intend to imply quality and accomplishment. It is certainly a far cry from the Cadillac ad of 1905 on page 157, in which a car is being driven up the steps of the Capitol building in Washington.

# THE PENALTY OF *Leadership*

*In every field of human endeavor, he that is first must perpetually live in the white light of publicity.    Whether the leadership be vested in a man or in a manufactured product, emulation and envy are ever at work.    In art, in literature, in music, in industry, the reward and the punishment are always the same.    The reward is widespread recognition; the punishment, fierce denial and detraction.    When a man's work becomes a standard for the whole world, it also becomes a target for the shafts of the envious few.    If his work be merely mediocre, he will be left severely alone—if he achieve a masterpiece, it will set a million tongues a-wagging.    Jealousy does not protrude its forked tongue at the artist who produces a commonplace painting.    Whatsoever you write, or paint, or play, or sing, or build, no one will strive to surpass or to slander you, unless your work be stamped with the seal of genius.    Long, long after a great work or a good work has been done, those who are disappointed or envious continue to cry out that it cannot be done.    Spiteful little voices in the domain of art were raised against our own Whistler as a mountebank, long after the big world had acclaimed him its greatest artistic genius.    Multitudes flocked to Bayreuth to worship at the musical shrine of Wagner, while the little group of those whom he had dethroned and displaced argued angrily that he was no musician at all.    The little world continued to protest that Fulton could never build a steamboat, while the big world flocked to the river banks to see his boat steam by.    The leader is assailed because he is a leader, and the effort to equal him is merely added proof of that leadership.    Failing to equal or to excel, the follower seeks to depreciate and to destroy—but only confirms once more the superiority of that which he strives to supplant.*

*There is nothing new in this.    It is as old as the world and as old as the human passions—envy, fear, greed, ambition, and the desire to surpass.    And it all avails nothing. If the leader truly leads, he remains—the leader.    Master-poet, master-painter, master-workman, each in his turn is assailed, and each holds his laurels through the ages.    That which is good or great makes itself known, no matter how loud the clamor of denial.    That which deserves to live—lives.*

America fell in love with this Jordan "Playboy" ad, "Somewhere West of Laramie." It smelled of prairie winds and open spaces. "Step into the Playboy and . . . start for the land of real living with . . . the lass who rides . . . into the red horizon of a Wyoming twilight." Advertising authorities still laud this ad and Cadillac's "Penalty of Leadership."

# Somewhere West of Laramie

SOMEWHERE west of Laramie there's a broncho-busting, steer-roping girl who knows what I'm talking about. She can tell what a sassy pony, that's a cross between greased lightning and the place where it hits, can do with eleven hundred pounds of steel and action when he's going high, wide and handsome.

The truth is—the Playboy was built for her.

Built for the lass whose face is brown with the sun when the day is done of revel and romp and race.

She loves the cross of the wild and the tame.

There's a savor of links about that car—of laughter and lilt and light—a hint of old loves—and saddle and quirt. It's a brawny thing—yet a graceful thing for the sweep o' the Avenue.

Step into the Playboy when the hour grows dull with things gone dead and stale.

Then start for the land of real living with the spirit of the lass who rides, lean and rangy, into the red horizon of a Wyoming twilight.

JORDAN MOTOR CAR COMPANY, Inc., Cleveland, Ohio

## Just Before the War, 1915

BETWEEN 1915 and 1916 the number of automobiles manufactured almost doubled. It went from 825,930 to 1,525,578, the greatest jump in the history of car production. In May of 1915 the great Cunard liner, the *Lusitania*, was torpedoed off the coast of Ireland, and 114 of the 1,153 men, women, and children drowned were Americans. Many thought that America's entry into the war was only a matter of weeks, and national attention was focused on the state of our armies and our armament. The Davidson-Cadillac Armored Car of 1915 (middle photo, left) showed the trend away from the armored car and toward our modern tank. The 1916 Armored Car (left, bottom), photographed on the Mexican border, had the high superstructure of a tank, was completely metal-encased, and mounted a circular gun turret.

The 1915 Flagler (top) was a $450 car manufactured in the small Michigan town of Cheboygan. It was a surprisingly light (900 lb.) cyclecar that enjoyed only a short life in the highly competitive days before the war. It was in 1916 that Oakland brought out one of the first V-8 motors, and the Roamer, advertised as "America's Smartest Car," boasted "Inherent Intrinsic Charm."

Pleasure or Commercial Car $450.00
F. O. B. Factory

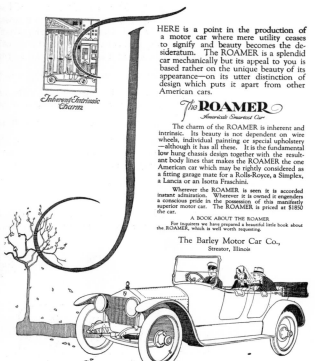

*Inherent Intrinsic Charm*

HERE is a point in the production of a motor car where mere utility ceases to signify and beauty becomes the desideratum. The ROAMER is a splendid car mechanically but its appeal to you is based rather on the unique beauty of its appearance—on its utter distinction of design which puts it apart from other American cars.

### The ROAMER
*America's Smartest Car*

The charm of the ROAMER is inherent and intrinsic. Its beauty is not dependent on wire wheels, individual painting or special upholstery —although it has all these. It is the fundamental low hung chassis design together with the resultant body lines that makes the ROAMER the one American car which may be rightly considered as a fitting garage mate for a Rolls-Royce, a Simplex, a Lancia or an Isotta Fraschini.

Wherever the ROAMER is seen it is accorded instant admiration. Wherever it is owned it engenders a conscious pride in the possession of this manifestly superior motor car. The ROAMER is priced at $1850 the car.

A BOOK ABOUT THE ROAMER
For inquirers we have prepared a beautiful little book about the ROAMER, which is well worth requesting.

The Barley Motor Car Co.,
Streator, Illinois

## Hughes in Rocky Mountains

The night of November 7, 1916, Charles Evans Hughes, Republican candidate for president, went to bed confident of victory. California voted heavily for Woodrow Wilson, however, and Mr. Hughes lost what appeared to be a certain victory. Mr. Hughes, the bearded gentleman in the rear seat, is pictured below in a 1916 White near Estes Park, Colorado.

## Gas Was High in 1916

The high price of gasoline produced this 1916 cartoon, which claimed men "starved and froze their families to keep 'er filled with gasoline . . . a gallon on the installment plan."

# Your Auto I. Q.

OF the 2,200 automobiles once made, only a few remain in our memories, and a mere handful are still manufactured today. The memory quiz below is essentially for the "old-timers" among us, those who grew up with the industry and like to be reminded of the early horseless-carriage days.

1. What eight cars were named after United States presidents?
2. What car borrowed the name of an American flower?
3. List five cars that were named after animals.
4. Eight cars, all defunct today, once had the names of states. What were they?
5. What three cars had the names of pictures on playing cards?
6. What car had the same name as a garden shrub?
7. What car borrowed the name of a heavy firearm?
8. What car had the name of a chirping insect?
9. What two cars had the names of birds?
10. What car had the name of a Victorian synonym for couch?
11. What car had the name of an imaginary reptile?
12. The car did not have fins, but it was named after a water creature. What was it?
13. What car had the name (slightly misspelled) of a man who clips hedges?
14. What two cars were named after breeds of dogs?
15. What two cars were named after United States generals, both of whom became presidents?
16. What car had the name of a very long race?
17. An English statesman and an Australian city had a car named after them. What was it?
18. What car had the name of the winner of the Battle of Austerlitz?
19. What car had the name of an American aviator and auto racer?
20. What car was named after the title given 96 of our elected representatives?
21. What car had the name of a famous Dutch painter and a type of beard?
22. What car had the name of a bed on wheels (and tracks)?
23. What three cars had the names of famous universities?
24. What car name was a synonym for windstorm?
25. What four cars had names that were the same as state nicknames?
26. What car was named after the head of an Indian tribe?

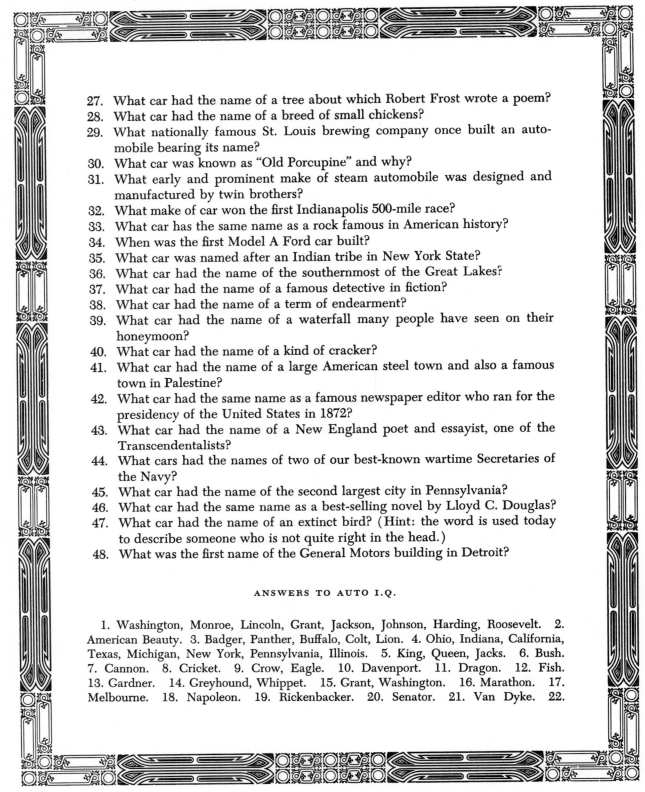

27. What car had the name of a tree about which Robert Frost wrote a poem?
28. What car had the name of a breed of small chickens?
29. What nationally famous St. Louis brewing company once built an automobile bearing its name?
30. What car was known as "Old Porcupine" and why?
31. What early and prominent make of steam automobile was designed and manufactured by twin brothers?
32. What make of car won the first Indianapolis 500-mile race?
33. What car has the same name as a rock famous in American history?
34. When was the first Model A Ford car built?
35. What car was named after an Indian tribe in New York State?
36. What car had the name of the southernmost of the Great Lakes?
37. What car had the name of a famous detective in fiction?
38. What car had the name of a term of endearment?
39. What car had the name of a waterfall many people have seen on their honeymoon?
40. What car had the name of a kind of cracker?
41. What car had the name of a large American steel town and also a famous town in Palestine?
42. What car had the same name as a famous newspaper editor who ran for the presidency of the United States in 1872?
43. What car had the name of a New England poet and essayist, one of the Transcendentalists?
44. What cars had the names of two of our best-known wartime Secretaries of the Navy?
45. What car had the name of the second largest city in Pennsylvania?
46. What car had the same name as a best-selling novel by Lloyd C. Douglas?
47. What car had the name of an extinct bird? (Hint: the word is used today to describe someone who is not quite right in the head.)
48. What was the first name of the General Motors building in Detroit?

### ANSWERS TO AUTO I.Q.

1. Washington, Monroe, Lincoln, Grant, Jackson, Johnson, Harding, Roosevelt. 2. American Beauty. 3. Badger, Panther, Buffalo, Colt, Lion. 4. Ohio, Indiana, California, Texas, Michigan, New York, Pennsylvania, Illinois. 5. King, Queen, Jacks. 6. Bush. 7. Cannon. 8. Cricket. 9. Crow, Eagle. 10. Davenport. 11. Dragon. 12. Fish. 13. Gardner. 14. Greyhound, Whippet. 15. Grant, Washington. 16. Marathon. 17. Melbourne. 18. Napoleon. 19. Rickenbacker. 20. Senator. 21. Van Dyke. 22.

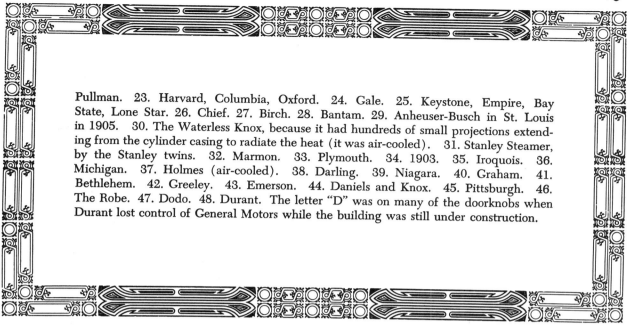

Pullman. 23. Harvard, Columbia, Oxford. 24. Gale. 25. Keystone, Empire, Bay State, Lone Star. 26. Chief. 27. Birch. 28. Bantam. 29. Anheuser-Busch in St. Louis in 1905. 30. The Waterless Knox, because it had hundreds of small projections extending from the cylinder casing to radiate the heat (it was air-cooled). 31. Stanley Steamer, by the Stanley twins. 32. Marmon. 33. Plymouth. 34. 1903. 35. Iroquois. 36. Michigan. 37. Holmes (air-cooled). 38. Darling. 39. Niagara. 40. Graham. 41. Bethlehem. 42. Greeley. 43. Emerson. 44. Daniels and Knox. 45. Pittsburgh. 46. The Robe. 47. Dodo. 48. Durant. The letter "D" was on many of the doorknobs when Durant lost control of General Motors while the building was still under construction.

## MY AUTO WITHOUT THEE,
## IN MONEY I WOULD BE

My auto, 'tis of thee,
Short cut to poverty—
　Of thee I chant.
I blew a pile of dough
On you three years ago,
Now you refuse to go—
　Or won't or can't.

Through town and countryside
I drove thee full of pride;
　No charm you lacked.
I loved your gaudy hue,
Your tires round and new—
Now I feel mighty blue,
　The way you act.

To thee, old rattlebox,
Came many bumps and knocks;
　For thee I grieve.
Badly thy top is torn;
Frayed are thy seats and worn;
The croup affects thy horn,
　I do believe.

Thy perfume swells the breeze,
While good folks cough and sneeze,
　As we pass by.
I paid for thee a price,
'Twould buy a mansion twice;
Now everyone yells "Ice"—
　I wonder why.

Thy motor has the grip;
Thy spark plug has the pip,
　And woe is thine.
I, too, have suffered chills,
Fatigue and kindred ills,
Trying to pay the bills
　Since thou were mine.

Gone is my bankroll now;
No more 'twould choke a cow,
　As once before.
Yet if I had the yen,
So help me John—Amen!
I'd buy a car again
　And speed some more.
　　　　　—Bay City Motorist

171

## In 1916, Convex Mudguards

In 1916 the United States girded for war, Henry Ford ventured into the tractor field, and the Lexington Minute Man Six (below) made much of their convex mudguards.

# CLASS

THE buyers of cars costing over $1,000 are demanding more and more of what is commonly called "class."

As a dealer you've got to recognize this fact if you stay in the running.

The LEXINGTON Minute Man Six **has class.**

The open touring model shows it, and the convertible model emphasizes it. Anybody can see it—except perhaps a dealer who is fighting a losing fight for a car whose makers have become set in their ways.

The makers of the LEXINGTON Minute Man Six are as close to the sources of motor car style as any men can be.

They are also builders of the LEXINGTON Thoroughbred Six ($2875) and know what ultra style and luxury mean. The building of LEXINGTON Thoroughbreds in the same shops raises the standards of workmanship throughout the LEXINGTON factory.

In the LEXINGTON Minute Man Six, class is combined with a price that is not prohibitive to the average car buyer. No wonder the LEXINGTON dealership is a franchise that is worth something!

Are you looking for such a connection? Write, wire— or better still, visit the factory and see for yourself.

**THE LEXINGTON-HOWARD CO. CONNERSVILLE, IND.**
1950 Columbia Avenue

## Lexington
### MINUTE MAN SIX

# Touring Car $1185

# Convertible Sedan $1350

**Lexington Salient Superiorities**
Lexington-Continental Engine
Moore Multiple Exhaust System
Cu Steel Starting Gear on Flywheel
Independent Ignition, Lighting, and Starting Circuits
Double Universal Joints
Full-Floating Rear Axle with Spiral Bevel Gears
Wick-Feed Oil Cups
Engine-Driven Tire Pump
Double Bulb Adjustable Headlamps Rigidly Mounted on Radiator
Largest Size Motometer
Bolted-on Tire Rack and Spare Demountable Rim
Oil Pressure Gauge
Convex Mud Guards
Genuine Leather Upholstery
In addition, the regular equipment includes full ventilating weather-stripped windshield, speedometer, electric horn, ammeter, and trouble lamp.

In 1917 the United States went to war, and auto production hit a new peak, 1,745,792 cars. There were enough cars to have plenty of wrecks, and in 1917 the first auto wrecker with crane made its appearance. The Hudson Super-Six Speedster (below) was a low and racy model with an excellent engine that drove it to several victories in the famous race up Pike's Peak. The 1917 five-passenger Buick D-6-45 (bottom) was finished in a color combination of green and black with a bronze stripe on the wheels. Many inveterate collectors turned their attention to automobiles about this time and chose radiator emblems (top, right) as a suitable item for collection.

## The Dodge Brothers, 1917

The Dodge Brothers, John and Horace, who started out in the automobile business as engine builders for Henry Ford and later filed suit against Ford, produced this unique and shiny two-door sedan with wire wheels in 1917 (bottom). In 1928 control of Dodge Brothers was purchased by Walter P. Chrysler. Below is a 1916 Cadillac Sedan with a V-8 engine and a glass partition between front and back seats, designed for use with a chauffeur.

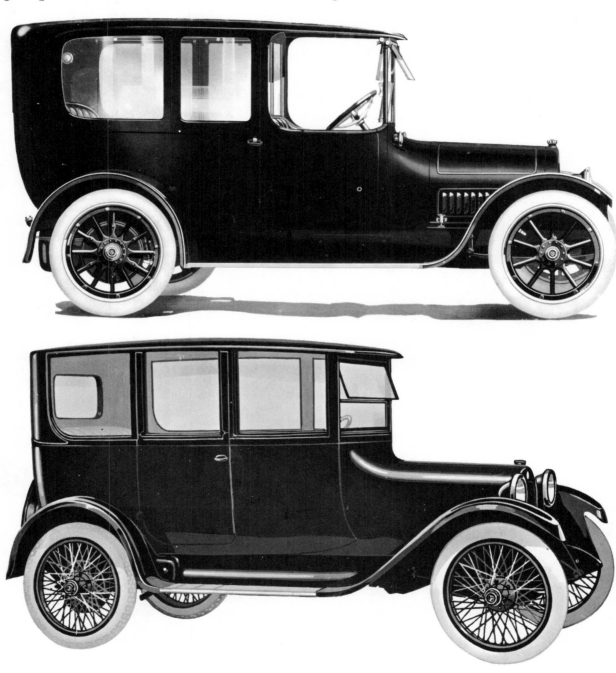

The 1917 Model T Coupe (below), with its high, towerlike cab, must have made the driver feel that he was indeed ruler of all he surveyed. By 1917 the Ford Model T was easily outselling all other makes, yet there were many who considered these glass-enclosed "showcases" a dangerous fad with no future. Despite occasional flying glass, the closed car was definitely here to stay.

Few people remember that the Chevrolet V-8 (bottom, left) preceded the Ford V-8. First manufactured in 1917, its special overhead valve mechanism supposedly made for "greater accessibility." The same engine (bottom, right) was also used by Oldsmobile for a time. Gaston and Louis Chevrolet were racing drivers of the Barney Oldfield era.

CHEVROLET

V-8 OVERHEAD VALVE ENGINE

175

## The Biddle, 1918

A golf caddy gazes admiringly at this sporty little 1918 coupé built by the Philadelphia Biddles. This artistic advertisement, with its country-club background, made a stir.

*Automobiles*
**BIDDLE**
*Speed*

The thrills of speed with perfect control are his who drives the Biddle car equipped with Deusenberg Motor. Security and comfort are also his – for the character of construction assures them

*Coach work – special types*

BIDDLE MOTOR CAR CO.
PHILADELPHIA, U.S.A.

The Doble-Detroit Company in 1918 thought it had produced the ultimate product in automobiles when it "harnessed the crude brute force of steam to . . . refining . . . electricity."

# Electrically Controlled Steam

For the first time the crude brute force of steam has been harnessed to the refining influence of electricity.

That is the big basic idea back of the Doble-Detroit Steam Car.

It is the differentiating factor between the Doble-Detroit and other steam propelled vehicles.

In the development of the gasoline car electricity has been the refining influence.

It is the one thing that makes possible the gasoline car in its present highly efficient state.

In the Doble-Detroit Car electricity plays the same vitally important part that it plays in the gasoline car.

It ignites the fuel and starts the car on the pressure of a button.

It makes possible a combustion chamber and generating system of marvelous compactness and efficiency.

It makes possible the use of kerosene or even lower grade and cheaper oil as the sole fuel—without any preheating or vaporizing devices.

It makes possible the automatic control of the steam pressure under varying operating conditions.

And—of course it furnishes an abundance of light for night driving.

In a word in the Doble-Detroit Car the use of steam is refined and simplified. Its efficiency is greatly increased. Its control is made amazingly simple and easy.

Again we want to emphasize that we firmly believe the Doble-Detroit to be the nearest approach to the Ultimate Car that has yet been achieved.

And we base this belief as we have already said upon the actual performance of Doble-Detroit Cars.

## Doble-Detroit Steam Motors Co.
### Detroit

177

# Things You Auto Know

The first De Soto was built in Auburn, Indiana, in 1913 and *not* by Chrysler. Since the inception of the industry, 125 different makes of steam automobiles have been built at various times in the United States. Cadillac is given credit for building the first car to have wheel steering, in 1902, although some say Packard was first.

White Steamers were once the official cars of the United States presidents. There was once a "Roosevelt" car, built by Marmon—before F.D.R. Two-cycle engines were very popular in early-day automobiles; they fired every time the piston went to the top of the cylinder and had only four moving parts—crankshaft, piston, connecting rod, and flywheel.

There were three Ajax cars built in the United States—an electric in New York City in 1901, one in Seattle, Washington, and the last Ajax (1923) by Nash. There were three cars named "Chicago." The Gale car, built in Galesburg, Illinois, had a tilting body to make it easier to work on the engine, located under the body. There was once a Hudson Steamer, built in 1901. Henry Ford once owned an imported Minerva, his personal car. Barney Oldfield once built cars bearing his name, in Los Angeles—1917 to 1922. There was also an Oldfield tire, made by Firestone. There was once a "Dan Patch" car, built in Minneapolis in 1911, a "Bugmobile" built in Chicago in 1907, and the "Seven Little Buffaloes" built in Buffalo, New York.

There was once a "Climber" car built in Little Rock, Arkansas, and a "Clymer," built in St. Louis, Missouri. Adolf Hitler may have promised a "People's" car, which he never delivered, but the "People's" car was built in 1901 at Cleveland, Ohio. There was a car built in Traverse City, Michigan, called the "Napoleon." The K.R.I.T., built in Detroit from 1909 to 1916, used a swastika as a trade-mark long before Hitler was ever heard of.

The "Greats" included the Great Arrow, Great Eagle, Great Smith, and Great Southern, and the last of the "Great" cars to go was the Great Western. The Carter Twin Engine car had *two* engines, each independent of the other (not the Cartercar). The Buckmobile was built in Utica, New York, in 1903. The "Air-Cooled" Chevrolet was actually a copper-cooled car with copper fins on the cylinders to radiate the heat. The first front-wheel-driven car was the Auto Fore Carriage, built in 1900 at New York City.

*The Saturday Evening Post* carried its first automobile advertising in 1900. In 1903 Buick built its original engine, a valve-in-head. The valve-in-head design has been a Buick feature ever since. The first Studebaker gasoline car was sold in 1904—previous to that time Studebaker built electric automobiles, and for a time after 1904 they built both gasoline and electric cars.

In 1906 L. L. Whitman drove an air-cooled Franklin from New York City to San Francisco in 15 days, 2 hours, 15 minutes—which was a new record. ☛ In 1909 Louis Chevrolet, a famous automobile racer, started building his six-cylinder overhead-valve engine in his machine shop on Grand River Boulevard in Detroit. ☛ After having built steam automobiles for several years, the White Sewing Machine Company built its first gasoline car in 1909. ☛ The first Buick "Six" was built in 1910.

In 1911 Reo established a new record from New York to San Francisco of 10 days, 15 hours, 13 minutes, cutting nearly four days off the previous record. ☛ In 1911 Buick built its first closed automobile. ☛ In 1912 Walter P. Chrysler started working as Works Manager of the Buick Motor Company under the direction of the late Charles W. Nash, who was then president of Buick. ☛ In 1913 Chevrolet moved to Flint, Michigan, and merged with the Little Motor Car Company. ☛ The Ford Motor Company built 1,000 cars a day for the first time in 1913.

In 1913 Chevrolet started building a four-cylinder car. They built a few V-8's later, in 1917 and early '18; then they built four-cylinder cars until 1929, when they came out with their "6." ☛ In 1922 Chevrolet built an air-cooled car, or, rather, displayed it at the Automobile Shows but made few, if any, sales. ☛ William C. Durant succeeded Charles W. Nash as president of General Motors Corporation in 1916. ☛ In 1917 the Nash car succeeded the Jeffery— from the first, Nash built a valve-in-head engine, probably on account of Mr. Nash's long association with Buick.

In 1919 Ralph DePalma established a new world's record of 149.8 miles per hour on the Florida beach in a Packard "905"; DePalma later came to Denver and gave an exhibition drive on Logan Street, in the heart of the residential section— he did over 100 miles an hour on this street, much to the amazement and excitement of the thousands of spectators who lined the sidewalks. ☛ In 1922 William S. Knudsen became vice-president of Chevrolet in charge of operations. ☛ In 1924 Winton, pioneer builder of automobiles, left the automobile field for Diesel engines.

Henry Ford startled the world in 1926 when he announced a five-day work week for employees. ☛ In 1925 Ralph Mulford covered 1,000 miles faster than anything on wheels had ever traveled before, when he drove a Chandler car that distance in 689 minutes. ☛ In 1927 Ford was out of production for six months during the period of the change from the Model T to the Model A Ford. However, the first Model A Ford was built in 1903. ☛ In 1929 Walter C. White and David Buick, pioneers of the automobile industry, passed away. ☛ In 1933 Ab Jenkins, former mayor of Salt Lake City, covered 3,000 miles in a Pierce-Arrow in less than 26 hours, a new and startling long-distance record.

## The Stanley Twins

THE Stanley brothers and the Smith brothers all had beards, and their contributions to American civilization—steam cars and cough drops, respectively—were considerable. Below are two photographs of the Stanley twins taken in exactly the same pose and spot but 20 years apart, in different steam cars of their own creation. The top photo is a formal shot of the two brothers, F. O. and F. E., in their first steam carriage in 1898. The bottom photo was taken in 1918 in a Stanley Touring Car of that year, just two months before F. E. Stanley was fatally injured in an automobile accident. F. O. Stanley died in 1940. At the very end of the century the Stanley brothers marketed only one steam car before they sold their business—factory, patents, parts, and good will—at a fancy figure to the Locomobile Company, which had been organized just for the purpose of buying out the Stanley brothers. One of the terms of the sale

was that the Stanleys could not make motor carriages for a period of two years. In 1901, however, at the expiration of this period, the Stanley brothers were manufacturing one of the finest horseless carriages in the country, a four-passenger car with a newly invented folding seat. Mr. F. O. Stanley was the first to drive a car, one of his steamers, to the top of Mount Washington, in 1899. The Stanley Steamer, unlike the Smith cough drop, is today extinct.

## Gasless Sunday, 1918

World War II was not the first conflict during which home-front motorists suffered. The cartoon below appeared in 1918. Even then it appears that motorists were plagued with gasless Sundays, rubber and steel shortages, high prices, high taxes, and lightless nights. It is interesting to compare car production figures for the two wars. In 1918, 943,436 cars were manufactured, about half the number made in 1917. In 1920 production jumped back to the 1917 level. In World War II our war effort was more "all-out." Production dropped in 1942 to one-tenth of its 1941 figure. From 1943 to 1945 no cars were marketed at all.

The Ford–General Motors competition existed even in 1918. Chevrolet offered this four-cylinder four-door Model 490 as competition for the Model T.

181

## Subdued Excellence, 1918—1919

Three very swank 1918–1919 models are pictured here. The Biddle ad (top), originally printed in full color, has no slogan, no guarantees, no announcements of new features—just the car and the name Biddle. The Cunningham uses the simple, well-modulated phrase, "Inspection invited." The Owen Magnetic (bottom) claimed to "banish the commonplace."

## Dempsey's Mammoth Machine

Jack Dempsey, former heavyweight boxing champion (below), drives a 1920 McFarlan, one of America's large and expensive cars. The 1915 Winton Six (bottom), "the closed car so necessary to a successful social season," speaks for itself with its top-hatted and furred passengers, flower vases, curtains, and chauffeur.

**WINTON SIX**

# The closed car, so necessary to a successful social season,

was never more superb in character and appointments than for the approaching winter.   Body types in variety and a wide range of color schemes and finishing fabrics, now ready for Winton Six buyers, assure exclusive beauty for your personal car, and lend a new charm to winter engagements.   It is not too late to place your order now.   The Winton Motor Car Co., 12 Berea Road, Cleveland, O.

*Branch Houses in Principal Cities*

## Electric Gearshift, 1920

This 1920 Premier had no gearshift lever, and shifting was done electrically by a lever on the steering quadrant. Early air-cooled Premier models gave way to water-cooled cars.

PREMIER is a fine, old, aristocratic family name. For more than a quarter of a century Premier motor cars have been among the best. Now comes a Premier —the finest of a fine line—a car so exclusive and so distinctive that, even among the finest cars you know, there is none with which it can be fairly compared.

For in no other car can you find an aluminum engine.

And the gears of no other car are shifted *electrically.*

The new Grecian body edge can be used by no other motor car.

All of which are mere superficial comforts and satisfactions.

When you get at the wheel of this car and drive it for one day—no one can ever weaken your fanatical devotion to it. You do not find the same POWER, the same smoothness, the same velvety road indifference in any other car—not even in the finest and most extravagant European Importations.

## PREMIER
MOTOR CORPORATION
INDIANAPOLIS····U·S·A
THE ALUMINUM SIX WITH MAGNETIC GEAR SHIFT

In the twenties—the "flapper" days—no sports roadster excelled the Kissel (top) for striking design and color. Painted bright yellow, it had a sloping windshield and a low, rakish body.

THE Kissel designing and construction policy interprets "custom-built" as a Fact —not a theory; a Practice— not a phrase.

In every detail of equipment —under-the-surface as well as on-the-surface—the most painstaking care is taken, not only to make each car complete, but of the custom-built quality and exclusiveness demanded by, and expected of, Kissel Tradition.

Three open and three closed custom-built models.

Kissel Motor Car Co.
Hartford, Wis., U. S. A.
*Originators of the ALL-YEAR Car.*

KISSEL *Custom-Built Six*

# I Grew Up with the Automobile

IF you were born at about the same time that the twentieth century was born, you were lucky enough to be a child about the time the automobile was a child. The two of you grew up together. I was such a child. In 1902 when I was seven, I fell in love with my father's curved-dash Oldsmobile. At ten I owned a single-cylinder Reo (bottom) and at eleven I was

YOUNG AUTO AGENT DEMONSTRATES MAXWELL

"the world's youngest automobile dealer" (left), in the words of President Theodore Roosevelt. I sold 26 cars my first 2 years. Other children in later years picked Red Grange and Babe Ruth for their heroes; I worshiped the men with wrenches and greasy hands: the Duryeas, the Stanleys, Ford, Olds, Oldfield, Buick, and the rest.

When I was fourteen and my brother Elmer eleven, we set out in a Flanders

186

"20" to drive from Denver to Spokane (right, top and bottom). We camped with cowboys and sheepherders, but somewhere in western Wyoming, the primitive paths and sandy trails proved too much for the Flander's rear end, and we gave up our adventure. Below, in

valve Harley-Davidson Racer. The same year, I won the first motorcycle race up Pike's Peak (14,108 feet), in 21 minutes, 15 seconds. I had, for the time being, fallen prey to the speed-record disease.

Racing is a young man's sport and I gave it up while I still had some un-

1946, those same two brothers (Elmer in uniform) alongside a 1912 Studebaker-Flanders.

At fifteen I drove a stripped, stock E.M.F. 1 mile in 1 minute and 10 seconds. In 1916 I set a world's Dirt-Track 100-mile record of 71 minutes on an 8-

broken bones. In 1921 I manufactured a windshield spotlight. All my life I have been collecting photos, clippings, and stories about automotive vehicles.

Still, the luckiest thing that ever happened to me was being born about the same time as the automobile.

187

## Custom-built Bodies, 1920

IN 1920 a fanatic desire for distinction and exclusiveness swept the automobile trade. The Don Lee organization of California catered to this fad by offering custom-built bodies (six of them are shown on these two pages) for mounting on any type of car.

*Touring Car for Mr. S. M. Spalding, of Beverly Hills, Calif., on Rolls - Royce Chassis.*

*Roadster for Mr. F. W. Mathison, of La Salle, Illinois, on Crane - Simplex Chassis.*

*Roadster for Mr. Roscoe Arbuckle, on Renault Chassis.*

188

*Touring Car for Mr. W. B. Schweppe, on Packard Chassis.*

*Touring Car for Miss Pauline Frederick, on Locomobile Chassis.*

*Two-Door Sedan, Mahogany Finished interior, on Cadillac Chassis, for Mr. Sussman Mitchell, of Visalia, Calif.*

189

# Cars Made in Cleveland

THE Buckeye State of Ohio provided competition for Michigan for a time in the making of automobiles. The following 82 makes of cars were once manufactured in Cleveland:

Abbott (P), 1918–1919
American (P), 1903–1905
Baker (P) and (T) (Electric), 1899–1919
Ben-Hur (P), 1916–1918
Berg (P), 1903–1912
Blakeslee (P) (Electric), 1906–1907
Brew-Hatcher (P), 1904–1905
Broc (P) and (T) (Electric), 1909–1915
Byrider (P) (Electric), 1908–1909
Buckeye (P), 1901
Chandler (P), 1913–1930
Clear & Dunham (P) (Electric), 1900
Cleveland (P) (Electric), 1900
Cleveland (P), 1902–1909
Cleveland (P) (Cyclecar), 1913–1914
Cleveland (T), 1912–1913
Cleveland (P), 1919–1927
Croxton (P), 1912–1913
DeMars (P) (Electric), 1905–1906
Denneed (T), 1916
Derain (P), 1910–1911
Disbrow (P), 1917–1918
Downing (P) (Cyclecar), 1914–1915
Durabile (P), 1902
Eastman (P) (Steam and Electric), 1901–1902
Ellwell-Parker (P) (Electric), 1908–1909
Euclid (P), 1908
Ewing (P) and (T), 1908–1910
Fedelia (P) (Cyclecar), 1913–1914
Ferris (P), 1920–1922
Gabriel (T) and (P), 1912–1918
Gaeth (P) and (T), 1902–1911
General (P) and (T), 1903–1904
Geneva (P) and (T) (Gasoline and Steam), 1901–1906
Globe (P), 1916–1919
Grant (P) and (T), 1916–1922
H.A.L. 12 (P), 1916–1918
Hanger (T), 1916
Hansen (P), 1902
Harding 12 (P), 1916–1917
Hoffman (P) (Steam and Gasoline), 1903–1904

Ideal (P) (Electric), 1906
Jordan (P), 1916–1931
Krastin (P), 1902–1903
Kurtz-Automatic (P), 1920–1923
La Marne (P), 1919–1921
Leon Rubay (P), 1922
Marsh (P), 1919–1921
Master (T), 1907
Merit (P), 1919–1922
Monarch (P), 1909
Moore (P), 1902–1903
Mora (T), 1910
Noble (P), 1902
Otto-Kar (P), 1904–1905
Owen (P), 1903
Owen-Magnetic (P), 1915–1922
Palmer (P), 1905–1906
Parsons (P) (Electric), 1905–1906
Paxon (T), 1911
Peerless (P) and (T), 1900–1932 (Steam and Gasoline)
People's (P) and (T), 1901
Phoenix (P), 1900–1901
Pomeroy (P), 1922
Rae (P) (Electric), 1905
Rauch & Lang (P) and (T), 1905–1924
Richard (P), 1914–1916
Rogers & Hanford (P), 1901
Rogers & Thatcher (P), 1903
Rollin (P), 1924–1927
Royal Tourist (P), 1903–1912
Russell (P), 1903–1904
Star (P), 1903–1904
Stearns (P), 1897–1916
Stearns-Knight (P), 1916–1930
Strong & Rogers (P) (Electric), 1900–1901
Stuyvesant (P), 1911–1912
Templar (P), 1918–1925
Unito (P), 1908–1910
White (P) and (T), 1901
Williams (P) (Electric), 1907–1908
Winton (P), 1897–1925

*(P) indicates passenger cars; (T) trucks.*

In 1920 a Cleveland make was this "small, superfine" Templar. The good-things-come-in-small-packages formula (small cars at high prices) did not intrigue the public for long.

*Templar*
(Reg. in U. S. Pat. Off.)

*The Superfine Small Car*

*The Pioneer Builder of Quality Small Cars*

Care which might seem overscrupulous is lavished on each Templar —and constantly evidenced in its performance.

Inbred worth and lasting luxury have won Templar ready repute as the finest small car in America. And Templar's fleet power, coupled with unusual economy of operation, has heightened this well-earned prestige.

Five-Passenger Touring, $2885
Four-Passenger Sportette, $2885     Two-Passenger Touring Roadster, $2885
Five-Passenger Sedan, $3785                Three-Passenger Coupe, $3785
*Prices f. o. b. Cleveland*

THE TEMPLAR MOTORS COMPANY
3000 Halstead Street, Lakewood, Cleveland, Ohio
Export Dept., 116 Broad St., New York City

## In 1920

In 1920, Americans sent to the White House two very ordinary John Q. Citizens, Warren G. Harding and Calvin Coolidge. The purchasing power of the 1914 dollar slipped to about 48 cents, business trends were all down, and everything from steel strikes to the approaching recession was blamed on the politicians. The car industry did not react to gloomy business predictions until later, however, and car production reached a new high in 1920 of 1,905,560.

The Bour-Davis Company of Shreveport, Louisiana, marketed an attractive car in 1915, and five years later produced this compact five-passenger touring car. In 1920 Henry Ford was temporarily $50,000,000 in debt owing to his program of expansion. The 1920 "Tin Lizzie" (below) put him back on his financial feet.

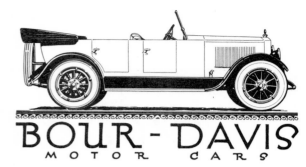

## BOUR-DAVIS
### MOTOR CARS

### The Reason for Bour-Davis Success

Bour-Davis Motor Cars have now been on the market for five years. They have proven an unqualified success. Wherever introduced they are popular rapid selling cars.

The reason for it is plain to anyone who has investigated the car.

It is a car without fads or radical features. It is built with a large percentage of reserve strength—with such close attention to detail—with such high quality parts all the way through that it has invariably satisfied its owners even though they have put it into service in the roughest sections of the country.

It is built in the south by men who know the extra severe service conditions to be met in the south and west.

Dealers in these sections will find it an ideal car to handle.

Short shipping distance—close proximity to the factory—a car that will stand an extra severe service—this is a combination which it is hard to equal.

We suggest that dealers who are interested write or wire for our dealer's proposition.

Our latest six color catalog will be sent on request

Export Offices: 100 Broad Street, New York

**DEALERS**
You will find the Bour-Davis an exceptionally profitable selling proposition. Some territory still open. Write for full information

**MODELS**
Five-Passenger Touring Car
Seven-Passenger Touring Car
Two-Passenger Roadster

LOUISIANA MOTOR CAR COMPANY · SHREVEPORT · LOUISIANA ·

In the early twenties cars shone with metal accessories and gadgets. Nickel-plated finish for lamps and radiators became standard, and many cars, like the 1921 Dodge (below, right) and the 1922 Paige (bottom), sported white side-wall tires. This Dodge also had a mirror on its left fender and Clymer spotlights through the windshield. The Paige Company advertised its 1922 model as "the most beautiful car in America."

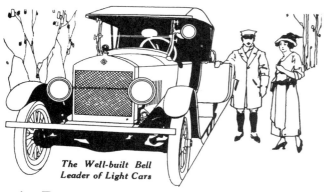

The Well-built Bell
Leader of Light Cars

## A Powerful—Yet Economical—Light Car With All The Comfort and Grace of A Heavy Car

THE Bell Car, in appearance, is as smart looking as it is mechanically efficient.

Simplicity is coupled with beauty—with due regard to utility, service and comfort.

The sturdiness of its chassis construction, the ease of its control, the soft cushioning of its spring structure, the responsiveness of its motor—all these qualities add to the comfort and safety of its performance on any roadway, on the steepest hills and crowded traffic.

The Bell appeals to the conservative buyer because it is a family car of high quality—distinctive appearance, complete in appointments and sells at a moderate price.

DEALERS: We still have some good territory open and would like to hear from a few live, reliable dealers and distributors. Write at once for our trade proposition.

**BELL MOTOR CAR COMPANY, Inc.**     **YORK, PA.**

Export Department, 100 Broad St., New York City

*The Bell Car is being exhibited in the lobby of the Majestic Hotel, 72nd Street and Central Park West, New York City.*

**$1,495**

Part of Bell Equipment:

Motor—Herschell-Spillman
Starter and Generator—Westinghouse
Carburetor—Stromberg
Steering Gear—Warner
Transmission—Muncie
Ignition—Atwater-Kent (for export — Simms Magneto)
Joints—Hartford
Axle—Peru
Bearing—Timken or Bower Roller

# BELL MOTOR CARS

## Essex and Buick, 1922

The revolutionary 1922 model of the Essex Coach (below)—a two-door, low-priced, four-cylinder car built by Hudson—created a stir because of its remarkable acceleration and top speed. The four-cylinder Buick (bottom) was manufactured as late as 1923.

The Stutz Bearcat (below) was one of the outstanding sports cars of the twenties. Usually painted a bright yellow, red, or blue, the Bearcat had a three-speed transmission mounted on the rear axle, cost $3,500, and was manufactured in Indianapolis.

Although several makes of light air-cooled cars are still being produced in Europe today, the air-cooled auto engine is a thing of the past in America. One of the best and last was the Franklin. Shown below, right, is an illustration of the air-cooling method used in a 1923 Franklin. A circular fan forced the air up, over, and down between the cylinders. The air-cooled engine was very light in weight. The Franklin Company advertised in 1923 that one of its air-cooled cars had been driven in the Imperial Valley of California for many hours in heat of 122 degrees "through trackless and uncharted seas of sand" with no dire results.

## B E A R C A T   R O A D S T E R

**D**ESCENDANT of a long line of illustrious champions of road and race course, the Stutz Bearcat Roadster preserves the best in Stutz traditions. The wealth of special equipment provided anticipates every need both of city driving and the tour. A trunk holding two suitcases and affording additional storage space; two extra rear-mounted tires and wheels; cowl and parking lights; heavy double spring bumper; distinctive plate glass windshield wings; adjustable cowl ventilator; rear vision mirror; automatic windshield cleaner, etc., are among the niceties afforded. Upholstery is in finest hand-buffed Spanish leather. Yellow, Royal Red, Azure Blue and Auto Brown painting are optional.

195

# My Merry Oldsmobile

SELDEN and Duryea and Ford had no idea what a boon the horseless carriage was going to be to the popular-song writers of the twenties. Since the beginning of the industry, songs have been written about the automobile and the motorist. In the early days the automobile also figured in many stage plays. At one time there were 29 shows in New York which were either built around the automobile theme or in which a car was actually brought on stage. The most famous auto song was Gus Edwards's "In My Merry Oldsmobile." The man most often mentioned in song was Henry Ford. "Poor Lizzie—What'll Become of You Now?" (opposite page) was published in 1928 when the Model T, or "Tin Lizzie," was being replaced by the Model A. The last line of this nostalgic and somewhat corny ballad is "Poor Lizzie, since Henry's done with you, what'll become of you now?" Another Ford song was "Henry's Made a Lady out of Lizzie" (below), which refers to the improvements in the Model A—"No More Bruises no more aches, now she's got those four-wheel brakes." "Get Out and Get Under" (opposite page) is another still remembered today:

> "A dozen times they'd start to hug and kiss
> And the darned old engine, it would miss.
> Then he'd have to get under, get out and get under, . . ."

## Henry's Made A Lady Out Of Lizzie

Talk of this and talk of that,
Boys you must take off your hat,
HENRY'S MADE A LADY OUT OF LIZZIE!
Has she plenty, has she much?
Got the "tin" you love to touch,
HENRY'S MADE A LADY OUT OF LIZZIE!
They used to park her in a lot,
For that they charged two bits,
But now they charge you nothing,
And you park her at the Ritz.
She once had rattles in her wheel,
But now she's full of "sex-appeal",
HENRY'S MADE A LADY OUT OF LIZZIE!

She's like all the other vamps,
Pretty shape and lovely lamps,
HENRY'S MADE A LADY OUT OF LIZZIE!
Since she's taken on some weight,
Honest, folks, she's looking great,
HENRY'S MADE A LADY OUT OF LIZZIE!
Her dash-board has a clock,
That's made a hit with all the Scotch,
A Scotchman saw the clock,
And so he promptly stopped his watch.
You've all heard the Frenchman song,
Fifty million can't be wrong,
HENRY'S MADE A LADY OUT OF LIZZIE!

Just a girl who knows her stuff,
Plenty fast but never rough,
HENRY'S MADE A LADY OUT OF LIZZIE!
Always tidy, always clean,
Faithful as an old Marine,
HENRY'S MADE A LADY OUT OF LIZZIE!
She's not the kind who tries to get
Your money all at once,
She only wants ten dollars down,
The rest in fourteen months,
Good for sister, nice for Ma,
Ev'rybody rides but Pa,
HENRY'S MADE A LADY OUT OF LIZZIE!

Ev'ry groom and blushing bride,
Now enjoy their buggy ride,
HENRY'S MADE A LADY OUT OF LIZZIE!
No one curses, no one swears,
Lizzie never needs repairs,
HENRY'S MADE A LADY OUT OF LIZZIE!
She used to kick and jump around,
On ev'ry trolley track,
But now she's very ladylike,
And never answers back.
She will surely catch your eye,
You know salesmen never lie,
HENRY'S MADE A LADY OUT OF LIZZIE!

No more chug-chug-chug-chug-bang!
No more cuss words, no more slang,
HENRY'S MADE A LADY OUT OF LIZZIE!
Not the noisy flapper kind,
Simply quiet and refined,
HENRY'S MADE A LADY OUT OF LIZZIE!
They used to say "We own a car,
It looks like one I mean",
But now they say "I'll have you know,
We own a Ford machine",
No more playing Jack and Jill,
No more tumbling down the hill,
HENRY'S MADE A LADY OUT OF LIZZIE!

When she's coming down the street,
All the boys say "Aint she sweet?"
HENRY'S MADE A LADY OUT OF LIZZIE!
Every man will go for her,
She's the kind that men prefer,
HENRY'S MADE A LADY OUT OF LIZZIE!
Why even Thomas Edison,
The wizard that he is,
Could not resist her charms,
And was the first to take out "Liz",
He said "She's Okay to me,
All she needs is company"
HENRY'S MADE A LADY OUT OF LIZZIE!

# I'm Wild About Horns On Automobiles That Go 'Ta-Ta-Ta-Ta

*by*
*Clarence Gaskill*

# POOR LIZZIE
## (WHAT'LL BECOME OF YOU NOW?)

*By*
*Abner Silver*
*and*
*Jack Meskill*

Irving Berlin Inc
MUSIC PUBLISHERS
1607 Broadway      New York

**BOBBY NORTH'S TERRIFIC HIT!**

# HE'D HAVE TO GET UNDER-
# GET OUT AND GET UNDER
## (TO FIX UP HIS AUTOMOBILE)

WORDS BY
GRANT CLARKE &
EDGAR LESLIE
MUSIC BY
MAURICE ABRAHAMS

MAURICE ABRAHAMS MUSIC CO.
1570 BROADWAY
NEW YORK

# THE LOVE STORY OF
# THE PACKARD AND THE FORD
### COMIC SONG

WORDS BY
HAROLD R. ATTERIDGE      HARRY CARROLL

MUSIC
PUBLISHERS
224 West 47th Street

197

# *1919* and *1924*

THE enormous, frightening, and formidable-looking vehicle at the left, top, was a 1924 Heine Velox manufactured in very limited numbers by the Heine-Velox Engineering Company in San Francisco. It had a twelve-cylinder engine, fender lamps, an inclined windshield set in rubber and was one of the first cars to have hydraulic brakes. The 1924 Eagle Car (top, right) was one of the many automobiles built, designed, or financed by W. C. Durant, of early General Motors fame. The 1919 Apperson (bottom) was a car for the elite fitted "to play its role in the elegant life with dignity and distinction." By 1924, balloon tires had become standard equipment and that year Ethyl gas was first introduced.

## APPERSON 8

### *The* EIGHT WITH EIGHTY LESS PARTS

IN the foreground of such scenes of elegant life one finds the Apperson playing its role with dignity and distinction. Fitted by appearance to mingle with the most expensive of imported productions. Powered to ask no favors in a friendly brush on the road with the swiftest cars built. Equipped with the powerful, responsive Apperson 8 Motor—the 8 with 80 less parts.

APPERSON BROTHERS AUTOMOBILE COMPANY, KOKOMO, INDIANA

The Apperson Anniversary Model Touring or Tourster
The Apperson Standard Model Touring or Sportster        Enclosed Models for Fall Delivery

198

In the early twenties steel disc wheels, like those on this 1923 Haynes, competed with wire wheels for popularity. The trunk for luggage at the rear was a forerunner of the enclosed luggage compartment used in the modern car of today.

THE NEW 1923 FIVE PASSENGER
HAYNES 57
SPORT TOURING

"NO EXTRAS TO BUY." The new, 1923 Haynes 57 Sport Touring Car answers most attractively the desire of the motorist for a typical sport model that shall be constantly serviceable and not simply for use on special occasions.

This five-passenger car comes fully equipped; everything accepted as an essential feature of a sport model is on the car; there are no "extras" to buy. Front and rear bumpers, polished protection bars and a spacious trunk in rear, six disc wheels with six cord tires and tubes, sun and vision visor, new design windshield wings, artistically fashioned individual steps, individual fenders and many other features which convey the impression of the last degree of quiet refinement and thoughtful design, are standard equipment.

Finished in a rich, Burgundy Wine color, resting on a 121-inch wheel base, powered by the famous Haynes-built light six motor, this newest Haynes is like an idealistic motor car brought into actual being at last.

Ask your Haynes dealer to demonstrate the four Haynes 57 Sport models, so that you may make your reservation immediately.

*We shall exhibit at the New York Automobile Show, Grand Central Palace, January 6 to 13, 1923.*

THE HAYNES AUTOMOBILE COMPANY, *Kokomo, Indiana*
EXPORT OFFICE: 1715 Broadway, New York City, U.S.A.

THE NEW, 1923 HAYNES 57 SPORT SEDAN, 5 PASSENGERS

THE NEW, 1923 HAYNES 57 SPORT COUPELET, 3 PASSENGERS

THE NEW, 1923 HAYNES 57 SPORT ROADSTER, 2 PASSENGERS

## From James Melton's Collection

Opera and radio singer James Melton is one of the many enthusiastic collectors of old automobiles who have, in following their avocation, done their country a great service. He owns one of the largest old car collections in the United States. Melton has restored the five cars on these pages to perfect running condition and has preserved them for future generations. Below are pictured a 1907 Locomobile with double-chain drive and a 1909 10-horsepower Stanley Steamer. On page 201, reading from the top, are a 1911 Peerless Victorian, a 1915 12-passenger Stanley Steamer Mountain Wagon, and a 1912 Pierce-Arrow "Vestibule Suburban."

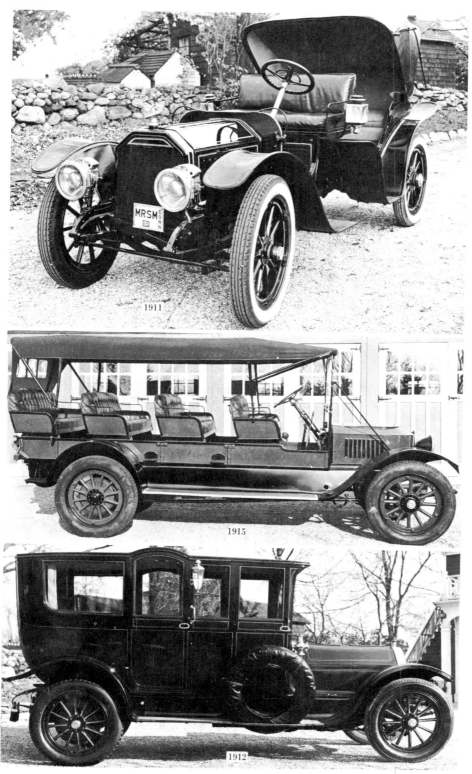

1911

1915

1912

## Walter P. Chrysler

The original Chrysler "70" (below, top) was the first car to bear its inventor's name, in 1924. Chrysler established himself by getting the Willys Overland Company out of the red in 1921, and then turned the same trick for the Maxwell and Chalmers Companies in the early twenties. Finally, in 1924, Chrysler started his own organization and three outstanding automotive men—Fred Zeder, Carl Breer, and O. R. Skelton—joined with him. Chrysler brought many innovations to the industry, including the high-compression engine, hydraulic four-wheel brakes, and rubber engine mountings. . . . Bottom, Ford's 1924 Model T.

202

# *Those Who Contributed*

These are the men who contributed the most to the invention, design, and production of American automobiles. Six of them are remembered today because there are still automobiles sold that bear their names: Chrysler, Dodge, Ford, Nash, Olds, and Studebaker. Some were primarily scientists and engineers, like Kettering, who invented the self-starter and developed Ethyl gasoline, or Leland of Cadillac, whose precision work led to the first automobile with interchangeable parts. Others were great financiers, executives, and organizers, like Durant, Joy, and Sloan. They were all men who devoted most of their lives to the automobile.

Picture courtesy Nash Motors—1946.

*(Seated at Table)*

**CHAPIN** — Prominent founding father of many automobile companies, including Hudson; with Henry Joy sponsored the program that gave America the world's best highways.

**CHRYSLER** — The Engineer and Great Innovator, who built an automotive empire by introducing many of today's widely adopted safety and comfort engineering features.

**DODGE**—John, and his brother Horace, expert machinists and consultants, contributed greatly to earlier cars and became famous makers in their own name.

**DURANT** — The Great Expansionist, whose daring plans brought vision to the infant industry, and orderly growth, financial strength, into the chaotic early years.

**DURYEA** — Charles, assisted by his brother Frank, built and demonstrated in 1892 the first successful gasoline car in America, and opened the first automobile factory.

**FORD** — The Great Idealist, courageous founder of the Ford Motor Company. First to show how prices could be lowered, wages increased, through modern assembly line production.

**HAYNES**—Outstanding Metallurgist and Inventor who, with the Appersons, Elmer and Edgar, figures prominently among the earliest of pioneer American automobile builders.

*(Standing left to right behind Table)*

**JOY**—The Great Believer in Detroit and the Lakes region as the coming industrial center of the world. Co-founder of Packard, he early established fame for American fine cars.

**KETTERING** —Inventor, Master Researcher; his efficient self-starter multiplied users for automobiles; worked with Thomas Midgley Jr., in the development of Ethyl gasoline.

**KING**—Inventor in many fields, first to drive a "Horseless Carriage" in Detroit. His proposal in 1895 led to the first association in America to promote the automobile industry.

**LELAND** — Master Mechanic, Engine Designer, whose close precision workmanship led to the first automobiles with interchangeable parts. Founder of Cadillac and Lincoln.

**MACAULEY** — Long leader of Packard; many times President of the Automobile Manufacturers Association; wartime President of the Automotive Council for War Production.

**MAXWELL** — The "Strong Right Hand" of many of the early Great, and Production Genius of his day. Renowned for establishing many production procedures.

**NASH** — The Great Organizer, who set several of today's well-known cars on an efficient basis, who founded Nash Motors and carried on the traditions of the famous Rambler cars.

**OLDS** — The Great Teacher —whose "Merry Oldsmobile" was a training school for many later famous car makers. First to put the automobile into large scale production.

**SLOAN** — The Great Executive, who has devoted a lifetime of service to the automotive industry, and who so capably has led General Motors for the past 23 years.

**STUDEBAKER** — Pioneer, engineer, who with his brothers formed a company whose fame spanned the transition period from fine carriages and wagons to present motor vehicles.

## Good Intentions, Bad Poem

The poet who dedicated this verse to the "Cars of Yesteryear" makes up in nostalgic enthusiasm what he lacks in poetic talent. Almost everyone likes to recall the "curious old gocarts."

### THE CARS OF YESTERYEAR!

How dear to my heart are the cars of my childhood
  When fond recollection presents them to view:
The "Chalmers," the "Rambler" around which men wild would
  Foregather and marvel at features quite new.
The wide-spreading "Knox" and the "White" that stood near it,
  The "Stevens," the "Pope" and the "Winton"—so swell,
    Those curious gocarts
    Those funny old slow carts
  Those plenty-of-dough carts that pleased me so well.

The old "E.M.F." that I hailed as a treasure,
  And often at night when I wanted a job
I found it a source of some pain and some pleasure
  To pilot the thing through a curious mob.
How ardent I seized it with hands that were glowing
  And scattered the folks with a musical bell—
    That noisy old boiler,
    That stubborn old boiler,
  That awkward old boiler I thought was so swell.

That 1910 "Bluebird" with side lamps enormous—
  It lit from a match if there wasn't a breeze;
That big starting crank with a book to inform us
  To "prime her a bit if she first tends to wheeze";
Those battleship headlights so huge but uncertain,
  Those Prest-O-Lite tanks which in fancy I smell—
    That 1910 buggy,
    So noisy and chuggy,
  That old-fashioned car long before prices fell.

How well I remember one old Stoddard-Dayton
  With big brassy gear shifts outside of the car;
It weighed sev'ral tons, but they called it a "phaeton"
  And when it went forth you could hear it 'afar.
An isinglass windshield it had, I remember—
  In summer it rolled up, in winter it fell—
    That old Stoddard-Dayton,
    That ponderous phaeton—
  That red Stoddard-Dayton that struck me as swell.

A grand old Pope-Hartford, an emblem of riches,
  I still can remember in front of the bank;
It never went far and 'twas often in ditches,
  But just to possess it meant money and rank;
It had a huge top which took three men to lower;
  Its two rubber horns scattered people pell-mell—
    That grand, old Pope-Hartford,
    That classy Pope-Hartford,
  That massive Pope-Hartford, distinctive and swell.

How dear to my heart are those cars of my boyhood,
  Things weren't too easy for them, you'll allow;
They thrilled my young heart as most any new toy would—
  But, frankly, I'm glad that they're not around now.
They ran on occasions; on others they didn't
  And whether you'd get home you couldn't foretell—
    Those old hossless wagons,
    Those early gas wagons,
  They're gone now forever and 'tis just as well.

FROM THE LOUISVILLE-JOURNAL AND TIMES

# MADE IN U.S.A.

APPROXIMATELY twenty-two hundred makes of cars were once manufactured in the United States. Most of these makes were born early in the history of the auto industry before mass production had set in and before it took such a large accumulation of capital to compete in the field. Many of the companies died an early death, and only one or two experimental models were made by some of the early manufacturers. Here is the most complete list of American cars yet accumulated, although research is still going on.

Numbers in parentheses after a car name indicate the number of cars bearing that name which were manufactured by different companies.

ABC (2)
Abbott
Abbott-Cleveland
Ace
Acme
Adams
Adams-Farwell
Adelphia
Adria
Advance
AEC
Aero
Aerocar
Aerotype
Ajax (Nash)
Ajax Electric
Akron
Alamobile
Aland
Alco
Alden-Sampson
Aldo
All-Steel
Allen
Allen-Kingston
Allith
Alma
Alpena
Alsace
Alter
Altha Electric
Ambassador
America
American (5)
American Bantam
American Electric
American Mercedes
American Mors
American Power Carriage
American Steam Car
American Steamer
American Tri-Car
American Underslung
Ames (2)

Amplex
Ams-Sterling
Anchor
Anderson (2)
Anger
Angus
Anhut
Anthony
Apollo
Appel
Apperson
Apple
Arbenz
Ardsley
Argo
Argo Electric
Argonne
Ariel
Aristos
Arrow Cyclecar
Artsberger Steamer
Atlantic Electric
Atlas
Atlas-Knight
Auburn
Aultman Steamer
Aurora
Austin (2)
Auto-Acetylene
Auto-Bug
Autocar
Auto Cycle
Auto Dynamic
Automatic
Automobile Fore Carriage
Automobile Voiturette
Automotor
Auto Tricar
Auto Two
Auto Vehicle
Avery

Babcock
Babcock Electric

Bachelles Electric
Bacon
Badger
Bailey
Baker Electric (2)
Baker Steamer
Balboa
Baldner
Baldwin Steamer
Ball
Banker
Bantam
Barbarino
Barley
Barlow Steamer
Barnes
Barrow Electric
Bartholomew
Bates
Bauer
Bay State (2)
Beardsley Electric
Beaver
Beggs
Belden
Bell (2)
Belmont (3)
Belmont Electric
Bendix
Benham
Ben Hur
Benner
Berg
Bergdoll
Berkshire
Berliet
Bertolet
Bessemer
Best
Bethlehem
Beverly
Bewis
Biddle
Biederman

Bimel
Binney and Bunham
Birch
Birmingham
Black
Black Crow (2)
Black Diamond
Blackhawk (2)
Blakeslee Electric
Bliss
BLM
Blomstrom
Blood
Boisselot
Bolte
Borbein Electric
Borland Electric
Boston and Amesbury
Boston High Wheel
Bour-Davis
Bournonville
Bowman
Bramwell
Bramwell-Robinson
Brasie
Brazier
Brecht Steamer
Brennan
Brew-Hatcher
Brewster
Briggs and Stratton
Briggs-Detroiter
Brightwood
Briscoe
Bristol
Broc Electric
Brock
Brodesser
Brook
Brooks
Brooks Steamer
Brown (2)
Brown Burtt
Brownell

205

# Made in U.S.A.

Brownie
Browniekar
Brush
Buckeye (2)
Buckles
Buckmobile
Buffalo
Buffalo Electric
Buffum
Buggycar
Bugmobile
Buick
Burdick
Burg
Burns
Burroughs
Bus
Byrider Electric

C.G.P.
Cadillac
California (2)
Californian
Calvert
Cameron (3)
Campbell
Canda
Cantono Electric
Capitol Steamer
Cardway
Carhart
Carhartt
Carlson
Car-Nation
Carrison
Carrol
Carroll
Cartercar
Carter Twin Engine
Cartermobile
Carthage
Case
Cato
Cavac
Cavalier
C-B
Centaur
Central
Century
Century Electric
Century Steam
Century Tourist
Chadwick
Chalfant
Chalmers
Champion (3)
Chandler
Chapman Electric
Charter Oak
Chase
Chelsea
Chevrolet
Chicago (2)
Chicago Electric
Chicago Steamer

Chief
Christie
Christman
Chrysler
Church (2)
Churchfield Electric
Cincinnati Steamer
Cinco
Cino
Clark
Clarke-Carter
Clark Electric
Clark Steamer
Clark-Hatfield
Clarksmobile
Classic
Clear and Dunham
Cleburne
Clermont (2)
Cleveland (3)
Climber
Cloughley
Club Car
Clyde
Clymer
Coates-Goshen
Coats Steamer
Cogswell
Coburn
Colby
Cole
Collinet
Collins Electric
Colonial (2)
Colonial Electric
Colt
Columbia (2)
Columbia Electric
Columbian Electric
Columbus (2)
Comet
Commander
Commerce
Commodore
Commonwealth
Compound
Conrad
Continental (4)
Corbin
Corbitt
Cord
Corinthian
Cornelian
Cornish-Friedberg
Correja
Corweg
Cosmopolitan
Cotta
Country Club
Courier (2)
Covert
Coyote
Craig-Hunt
Craig-Toledo
Crane

Crane and Breed
Crane-Simplex
Crawford
Crescent (2)
Crestmobile
Cricket
Criterion
Croesus
Crompton
Crosley
Crouch
Crowdus Electric
Crow-Elkhart
Crown (2)
Crowther-Duryea
Croxton
Croxton-Keeton
Cruiser
Crusader
Cull
Culver
Cunningham
Cunningham Steamer
Cutting
C.V.I.
Cycleplane

D.A.C.
Dagmar
Dalton
Daniels (2)
Dan Patch
Darby
Darling (2)
Darrow
Dart
Davenport
Davis (2)
Dawson
Day
Day Electric
Dayton
Dayton Electric
Deal
Decauville
Decker
De Cross
Deere
Deering Magnetic
De La Vergne
Delling Steamer
Dellmore
Deltal
De Luxe
Demotcar
De Motte
De Rain
Desberon
De Soto (2)
De Tamble
Detroit (3)
Detroit-Chatham
Detroit-Dearborn
Detroit Electric
Detroit-Speedster

Detroit Steamer
Detroiter
De Vaux
Dewabout
Diamond
Diamond Arrow
Diamond T
Diana
Dile
Disbrow
Dispatch
Dixie (2)
Dixie Flyer
Dixie Tourist
Dodge
Dodgeson
Dodge Steam Car
Dolson
Dorris
Dort
Douglas
Downing
Downing-Detroit
Dragon
Drake
Drexel
Driggs
Drummond
Dudley
Duer
Duesenberg
Dumont
Dunn
Duplex
DuPont
Duquesne
Durant
Durocar
Duryea
Dusseau
Dyke
Dymaxton
Eagle (5)
Eagle Electric
Eagle Rotary
Earl (2)
Eastman Electric
Eaton Electric
Eck
Eclipse Steamer
Economy (2)
Economycar
Eddy Electric
Edwards-Knight
E.H.V.
Eichstaedt
E.I.M.
Elbert
Elcar
Elco
Eldredge

Electra
Electronomic Steamer
Elgin

Elinore
Elite
Elite Steamer
Elkhart
Elliott
Ellis Electric
Ellsworth
Elmore
Elwell-Parker
Emancipator
Emerson (2)
E.M.F.
Empire (2)
Endurance Steamer
Englehardt
Enger
Engler
Entyre
Entz
Erie (2)
Erskine
Essex
Essex Steamer
Euclid
Eureka (2)
Evansville
Everitt
Everybody's
Ewing

Fageo
F.A.L.
Falcon (2)
Falcon-Knight
Famous
Fanning
Farmack
Farmobile
Farner
Federal
Federal Steamer
Fenton
Fergus
Ferris
Findley
Firestone-Columbus
Fischer
Fish
Fisher
Flagler
Flanders
Flanders Electric
Flexbi
Flint (3)
Flyer
Ford
Forest
Fort Pitt
Foster Steamer
Fostoria (2)
Fox
Frankfort
Franklin
Frayer
Frayer-Miller

Frederickson
Fredonia
Fremont
French
Friedman
Friend
Fritchie Electric
Frontenac (3)
Frontmobile
F.R.P.
F.S.
Fuller (2)
Fulton
F.W.D.
Fwick

Gabriel
Gadabout
Gaeth Steamer
Gale
Gardner
Garford
Gas-au-lec
Gasmobile
Gaylord
Gearless
Gearless Steamer
Gem
General
General Electric
Genesee
Geneva
German-American
Geronimo
Gersix
Ghent
Gibbs Electric
Gibson
Gillette
G.J.G.
Gleason
Glide
Globe
Glover
Goethe
Goldeneagle
Goodspeed
Grabowsky
Graham (2)
Graham-Paige
Gramm
Grand
Granite Falls
Grant
Graves-Condon
Gray
Great Eagle
Great Smith
Great Southern
Great Western
Greeley
Gregory
Grensfelder
Greuter
Greyhound

Grinnell Electric
Griswold
Grout
Gurley
Gyroscope

Hackett
H.A.L.
Hall
Halladay (2)
Hambrick
Hamilton
Hamlin-Holmes
Hammer
Handley
Handley-Knight
Hanover
Hansen
Hanson
Harding
Hardy
Harper
Harrie
Harrigan
Harris
Harrison
Harroun
Hart-Kraft
Hartley Steamer
Hartman
Harvard
Hasbrouck
Haseltine
Hassler
Hatfield (3)
Havers
Hawley
Hayberg
Haydock
Haynes
Haynes-Apperson
Hayward
Hazard
H.C.S.
Healy Electric
Hebb
Heifner
Heilman
Heine-Velox
Hendel
Henderson
Henney
Henrietta Steamer
Henry
Hercules (2)
Herff-Brooks
Herreshoff
Hertel
Hertz
Hess Steam
Hewitt
Hewitt Lindstrom
Heyman(n)
Hicks
Highlander

Hill
Hines
Hobbie
Hoffman
Hoffman Steamer
Holden
Holland
Holley
Hollier
Holly
Holmes (2)
Holsman
Hol-Ten
Holyoke (2)
Homer Laughlin
Hoosier Scout
Hopkins
Hoskins
Houghton
Houghton Steamer
Houpt
Houpt-Rockwell
House Steamer
Howard (3)
Howey
Hudson
Hudson Steamer
Huffman
Hunter
Hupmobile
Hupp-Yeats Electric
Hydrometer

Ideal (4)
Ideal Electric
Illinois Electric (2)
Imp
Imperial (2)
Imperial Electric
Independence
Independent
Indianapolis
Ingrame-Hatch
Innes
International
International Gasoline Carriage
Inter State
Intrepid
Iroquois
Iverson
Izzer

Jackson
Jack's Runabout
Jacquet
James
Janney
Jarvis-Huntington
Jaxon Steamer
Jeffery
Jem
Jenkins
Jewel
Jewett

# Made in U.S.A.

Johnson
Johnson Steamer
Jones
Jones-Corbin
Jonz
Jordan
J.P.L.
Julian
Junior

Kalamazoo
Kane-Jennington
Kankakee
Kansas City
Kato
Kauffman
K.D.
Kearnes
Keene Steamobile
Keeton
Keller-Kar
Kellogg Steamer
Kelsey (3)
Kenmore
Kennedy
Kensington Steamer
Kent
Kenworthy
Kermath
Kermet
Kerosene Motor Surrey
Keystone
Keystone Steamer
Kiblinger
Kidder
Kimball Electric
King
Kinn(e)ar
Kirk
Kissel (Kar)
Kleiber
Kline(Kar)
Klink
Klock
Knickerbocker
Knight Special
Knox
Koehler
Komet
Konigslow
Koppin
Kraft Steamer
Kreuger
K.R.I.T.
Kunz
Kurtz

Laconia
Lad's Car
Lafayette (2)
LeMarne
Lambert
Lancamobile
Lane Steamer
Lanpher

Lansden Electrette
La Petite
Larchmont Steamer
Larson
La Salle
Laurel
Lauth Jergens
L. C. Erbes
L. & E.
Leach
Leach-Biltwell
Leader
Lehr
Lende
Lenox
Lenox Electric
Lescina
Lewis (2)
Lexington
Liberty
Lima
Lincoln (2)
Lin(d)sley
Lion
Little
Little Mac
Locomobile
Logan
Lomax
Lone Star
Long
Longest
Loomis
Lorraine (2)
Los Angeles
Louisiana
Lowell-American
Lozier
Lozier Steamer
L.P.C.
Lueding Haus
Lutz Steamer
Luverne
Lyman
Lyman-Burnham
Lyon
Lyons-Atlas
Lyons-Knight

Maccar
MacDonald Steam Car
Mackle-Thompson
Macomber
Macon
Madison
Magic
Magnolia
Mahoning
Maibohm
Majestic
Malcolm
Malcolm-Jones
Malden-Steamer
Manexall
Manistee

Maplebay
Marathon
Marble Swift
Marion
Marion-Handley
Mark Electric
Marlboro Steamer
Marmon
Marquette (2)
Marr
Marsh (2)
Marshall
Martin (2)
Martin-Wasp
Marvel
Maryland
Mason
Mason Steamer
Massilon
Master
Matheson
Mathews
Maxim-Goodridge Electric
Maxwell
Maxwell-Briscoe
Mayer
Mayfair
Maytag
McCue
McCullough
McCurdy
McFarlan
McGill
McIntyre
McKay Steamer
Mead
Mecca
Med-Bow
Media
Mel Special
Menges
Mercer
Mercury (3)
Merit
Merkel
Merz
Meteor
Meteor Steamer
Metropol(e)
Metropolitan
Metz
Metzger
Michigan
Middleby
Midgley
Midland
Midwest
Mier
Milac
Milburn Electric
Militaire
Miller
Milwaukee Steamer
Minneapolis
Mino

Mitchell
Mitchell-Lewis
Mobile Steamer
Model
Modoc
Mogul
Mohawk
Moline (2)
Moline-Knight
Moller
Monarch (2)
Moncrief(f)
Mondex-Magic
Monitor
Monroe
Moody
Mooers
Moon
Moore (2)
Mora
Morgan
Morris(s)
Morris & Salom
Morris-London
Morse (2)
Motorette
Moyea
Moyer
M.P.M.
Mueller-Benz
Mulford
Multiplex
Muncie
Murdaugh
Murray
Murray-(Mac)
Mutual

Nance
Napier
Napoleon
Nash
National
National Electric
Neilson
Nelson (2)
Neustadt-Perry
Newark
New England Steamer
New Era
New Home
New York
Niagara (2)
Nichols Shepard
Noble
Noma
Northern
Northway
Northwestern
Norton
Norwalk Underslung
Novara
Nyberg

Oakland

Oakman-Hertel
Obertine
Ogren
Ohio Electric
Ohio Falls
Okey
Oldfield
Oldsmobile
Olympian
Omaha
Omar
Only
Orient
Ormond Steamer
Orson
Otto
Ottoker
Ottomobile
Overland (2)
Overholt
Overman Steamer
Owen
Owen Magnetic
Owen Shoeneck
Owen Thomas
O-We-Go
Oxford

Pacific
Packard
Page
Page-Toledo
Paige
Paige-Detroit
Palmer
Palmer-Moore
Palmer-Singer
Pan
Pan-Am
Pan-American
Panther
Paragon (2)
Parenti
Parry
Parsons-Electric
Partin-Palmer
Paterson
Pathfinder
Patterson-Greenfield
Pawtucker Steamer
Payne-Modern
Peerless
Penn
Pennsy
Pennsylvania
People's
Perfection
Perfex
Peru
P.E.T.
Peter Pan
Peters
Petrel
Phelps
Phianna

Phipps Electric
Phoenix
Pickard
Piedmont
Pierce-Arrow
Pierce-Racine
Pilgrim
Pilliod
Pilot
Pioneer
Piscorski
Pittsburgh
Pittsburgh Electric
Planche
Plymouth (2)
Pneumobile
Pomeroy (2)
Ponder
Pontiac (2)
Pope
Pope-Hartford
Pope-Robinson
Pope-Toledo
Pope-Tribune
Pope-Waverley
Poppy-Car
Porter
Port Huron
Porter Steamer
Portland
Postal
Power-Car
Prado
Pratt-Elkhart
Premier
Premocar
Prescott Steamer
Preston
Pridemore
Primo
Princess
Prospect
Pullman
Pungs-Finch
Puritan Steamer

Queen
Quick

Rae
Railsbach
Rainier
Raleigh
Rambler
Randall
Randall Steamer
Randolph
Ranger (2)
Rapid
Rauch & Lang Electric
Raulang Electric
Rayfield
R-C-H
Read
Reading

Reading Steamer
Real
Reber
Red Bug
Red Jacket
Rees
Reeves
Regal
Regas
Reinertsen
Reliable Dayton
Reliance
Remal-Vincent Steamer
Remington
Reo
Republic
Re Vere
Rex
Rhodes
Ri Chard
Richelieu
Richmond
Rickenbacker
Ricketts
Riddle
Rider-Lewis
Riess-Royal
Riker Electric
Riley & Cowley Steamer
Riper
Ritz
Riveria
R-O
Roader
Roamer
Robe
Robie
Robinson
Robson
Roche
Rochester Steamer
Rocket
Rock Falls
Rockne
Rockway
Rockwell
Rodgers
Roebling
Rogers (2)
Rogers & Hanford
Rogers Steamobile
Rollin
Rolls Royce
Roman
Romer
Roosevelt
Roper Steamer
Ross
Ross Steamer
Rotary (2)
Rovena
Royal
Royal-Tourist
Rubay
Rush

Rushmobile
Russell
Ruxton
R & V Knight

Saginaw
Salter
Sampson
Sandusky
Santos Dumont
Savage
Saxon
Sayers
Schacht
Scott
Scott-Newcomb Steamer
Scripps-Booth
Seagrave
Searchmont
Sears
Sebring
Sekine
Selden
Sellers
Senator
Seneca
Serpentina
Serrifile
Seven Little Buffaloes
Severin
S.G.V.
Shad-wyck
Shain
Sharon
Sharp-Arrow
Shaum
Shaw
Shawmut
Shelby
Sheridan
Shoemaker
Sibley
Sibley-Curtis
Signet
Silent
Silent Knight
Silver Knight
Simms
Simplex
Simplicity (2)
Simplo
Singer
Single Center
Sintz
S.J.R.
Skelton
Skene Steamer
S & M
Smith & Mabley Simplex
S-N
Snyder
Sommer
Soules
Southern
Sovereign

209

# Made in U.S.A.

Spacke
Spartan
Spaulding (2)
Special
Speedway
Speedwell
Spencer
Spencer Steamer
Sphynx
Spoerer
Springer
Springfield
Sprite Cyclecar
Squier Steamer
S.S.E.
Stafford
Stammobile Steamer
Standard (4)
Standard-8
Standard Electrique
Standard Steamer (2)
Stanley (2)
Stanley Steamer
Stanley Whitney
Stanton Steamer
Stanwood
Star (2)
Starin
States
Static Super
Staver
Steamobile
Stearns
Stearns-Knight
Stearns Steam
Steco
Steel Swallow
Steinhart Jensen
Steinmetz
Stephens
Sterling (3)
Sterling-Knight
Stetson
Stewart
Stewart-Coates
Stevens-Duryea
Stickney-Motorette
Stilson
St. Joe
St. Louis
Stoddard

Stoddard-Dayton
Storck
Storms Electric
Stout Scarab
Strathmore Steamer
Stratton
Streator
Stringer Steamer
Strobe & Martin
Strouse
Studebaker
Studebaker Electric
Studebaker-Garford
Sturgis Electric
Sturtevant
Stutz
Stuyvesant
Suburban
Success
Sultan
Summit
Sun
Sunset
Superior
Supreme
Synnestvedt
Syracuse Electric

Tarkington
Taunton Steamer
Templar
Templeton-Dubrie
Tex
Texan
Texmobile
Thomas
Thomas-Detroit
Thompson
Thorobred
Thresher Electric
Tiffany
Tiffin
Tiger
Tincher
Tinkham
Toledo Steamer
Tonawanda
Torbensen
Touraine
Tourist
Traveler (2)

Trebert
Tribune
Trimo
Trimoto
Trinity Steamer
Triumph
Trumbull
Tulsa
Twincity
Twombly
Twyford

Union
United
Universal
Upton
U.S.
U.S. Electric
U..S Long Distance

Van
Van-L
Van Dyke
Van Wagoner
Vaughan (3)
V.E.
Velie
Vernon
Vestal
Victor (2)
Victor Steamer
Victory
Viking (2)
Vixen
Vogue
Voiturette
Vulcan

Waco
Wagenthals
Wahl
Waldron
Walker
Walls
Walter
Waltham
Waltham Orient
Walther
Walworth
Ward
Ward Electric
Warren

Warwick
Washington (3)
Wasp
Waterloo
Watrous
Watt
Waukesha
Waverley Electric
Wayne
Welch
Westcott
Westfield
W.F.S.
Whaley-Henriette
Wharton
Whippet
White
White Hickory
White Steamer
White Star
Whiting
Whitney Steamer
Wick
Wilcox
Wildman
Williams Electric
Wills-Sainte Claire
Willys
Willys-Knight
Willys-Overland
Windsor
Wing
Winther
Winton
Wizard
Wolfe
Wolverine (2)
Wonder
Woodruff
Woods
Woods Dual Power
Woods Mobilette
Worth

Yale (2)
Yates
York

Zent
Zentmobile
Zimmerman
Zip

This book has spanned the period from 1877, the year that George P. Selden invented his first automobile, to 1925. By the mid-twenties mass production, specialization, and assembly lines had increased automobile production well into the millions. Competition was keen and many good and well-known makes were forced out of business. It required, and requires today, an enormous amount of capital to stay in the automobile business.

Although the day of the automobile pioneer is over, this book is meant as a very humble and admittedly inadequate tribute to those early inventors and engineers who first put America on wheels.

INDEX ☞

# INDEX

213